THE

BRONTËS IN IRELAND

Or, Facts Stranger than Fiction

BY

Dr. WILLIAM WRIGHT

HASKELL HOUSE PUBLISHERS LTD.
Publishers of Scarce Scholarly Books
NEW YORK. N.Y. 10012
1971

First Published 1893

HASKELL HOUSE PUBLISHERS LTD.
Publishers of Scarce Scholarly Books
280 LAFAYETTE STREET
NEW YORK, N. Y. 10012

Library of Congress Catalog Card Number: 70-160161

Standard Book Number 8383-1237-8

Printed in the United States of America

Printing Statement:

Due to the very old age and scarcity of this book,
many of the pages may be hard to read due to the
blurring of the original text, possible missing pages,
missing text and other issues beyond our control.

Because this is such an important and rare work, we
believe it is best to reproduce this book regardless of
its original condition.

Thank you for your understanding.

PATRICK BRONTË'S BIRTHPLACE.

BRONTËS IN IRELAND

PREFACE

I TRUST it is unnecessary to say that I disclaim all responsibility for the Brontë acts, opinions, and sentiments recorded in this book. As no one living could lay claim to Brontë genius, even in its less-cultured condition, no one should be held responsible for the eccentricities of that genius.

It is right, however, that I should express my indebtedness to many for generous encouragement and unstinted assistance in setting in order these fragments of an almost forgotten past.

In a very special manner I have to acknowledge my obligation to Dr. W. Robertson Nicoll, whose sympathy with the Brontë genius is as profound as his knowledge of the literature is unrivalled. Dr. Nicoll has the rare power of kindling the zeal of others at his own torch, and but for his enthusiasm the story of *The Brontës in Ireland* would probably never have been published.

The Rev. J. B. Lusk, M.A., now resident in the

PREFACE

Ballynaskeagh manse, has been indefatigable in investigating old documents, and in interviewing old residents, and generally in verifying my accumulated facts. Besides enabling me to study the history of the Brontës from new standpoints, he has disposed for ever of the baseless assertion that the family was called " Prunty " in Ireland.

The Rev. W. John McCracken of Ballyeaston, Belfast, who knew the Brontës personally, has placed at my disposal, in written form, his recollections of the family.

The Rev. R. H. Harshaw of Mount Mellick, in whose grandfather's house Hugh Brontë was once a hired servant, has kindly supplied me with valuable details.

The Rev. H. W. Lett, Rector of Aghaderg, Loughbrickland, to whom we owe the recovery of the Drumgooland Vestry-book, has generously given me permission to make use of his summary of that precious document.

I am much indebted to the Registrar of Cambridge University, and to the Bursar of St. John's College, for information readily and courteously given. They have shown that there was no trace of the name of " Prunty " at Cambridge, as Mr.

PREFACE

vii

Lusk has shown that there was no trace of it in Ireland.

From Miss Ellen Nussey, the " Miss E." of the Gaskell biography, and the Caroline Helstone of *Shirley*, I have heard abundant details regarding the gifted family in England. Miss Nussey is a close observer and a vivid narrator, and during a much-appreciated visit to my house in April 1891 she often made the inmates of the Haworth vicarage live again.

Besides Miss Nussey, several other ladies helped me much ; and to many in humble life in Ireland I am deeply indebted for information regarding matters which had fallen within their own observation.

When my many helpers discover in these pages little trace of the abundant material which they placed at my disposal, I trust they will remember that the narrative had to be kept within narrow limits, and that every bit of information helped me to come to conclusions on doubtful matters, and contributed to the general result. Besides, there are several important incidents which I have left untold, believing as I do that in such matters the half is more than the whole.

viii *PREFACE*

I must also thank my spirited publishers on both sides of the Atlantic for the attractive form in which they have brought out the book.

While acknowledging my great indebtedness to the living, I must admit that my obligation to the dead is still greater.

WILLIAM WRIGHT.

WOOLSTHORPE, NORWOOD,
October 1893.

CONTENTS

CHAPTER I.

PAGES

THE HIDDEN SOURCES . . . . .

The history of the Brontës and the history of the Nile—Investigations mainly on English soil—Guess-work—The heart of the mystery in Ireland—Mrs. Gaskell's tribute inadequate—Something beyond Mr. Wemyss Reid's theory—Mr. Augustine Birrell's additional facts and pointless sarcasm—Authors building on an Egyptian model—Mr. Erskine Stuart's prediction.

CHAPTER II.

THE CHIEF SOURCES OF INFORMATION: PRE-LIMINARY . . . . . . 6—14

Exceptional advantages for telling the tale—My nurse's tales—My tutor's recollections—His methods—Early screeds of Brontë novels—The grain of truth in Bran-well's boast—The facts of *Wuthering Heights*—The Todds and McAllisters—Rev. David McKee, the friend and adviser of the Brontës—The novels first read in his manse—Arrival of *Jane Eyre*—Side lights—Collecting facts.

CHAPTER III.

GRANDFATHER BRONTË'S EARLY HOME . 15—18

Hereditary gift of story-telling—Miss Ellen Nussey's testimony—The girls hanging on their father's lips—Grandfather Brontë and *Jane Eyre*—Hugh's childhood—An uncle and aunt arrive—Laying plans—Visions of paradise—A night to be remembered—Incidents remembered — The dressmaker's *beverage* — Last adieux from brothers and sisters—His mother's caresses—Out in the darkness.

ix

CONTENTS

CHAPTER IV.

THE FOUNDLING AND FOSTER-FRIENDS . . 19—31

PAGES

The great-great-grandfather of the novelists—Home near Drogheda on the Boyne—Dirty child found on a boat from Liverpool to Drogheda—Mrs. Brontë and the infant —Baby taken home and called Welsh—Brontës golden-haired from the third generation—Welsh's unhappy lot—Meets cruelty by cunning—Clings to great-great-grandfather Hugh—Accompanies him to fairs and markets—The little spy useful—The successful cattle-dealer—Mysterious death of great-great-grandfather Hugh—Position of the family—Conference with Welsh—Welsh proposes to marry Mary Brontë, his late master's daughter —Rejected with scorn—Welsh's threat—Action of the family—Counter-action of Welsh—A land agent and entourage—Welsh a sub-agent—His business—Helps himself as well as his master--His twofold purpose--Meg a female sub-agent—Her functions—Courtship by proxy—The constant drip—Welsh meets Mary Brontë and carries out his designs—Marriage in secret, proclaimed on the housetops—Welsh secures the farm--The brothers and the agent—Law and order—Birth of the tenant-right theory.

CHAPTER V.

THE ADOPTION AND OATH . . . . 32—34

Eviction and vengeance—Burning of the old home—Welsh's repentance—Official oaths and family oaths—The lost clue.

CHAPTER VI.

A FEARFUL JOURNEY . . . . . 35—50

Welsh without the mask—A child's struggle in the dark —A curse and a blow—Dreaming of home—The careless heavens—Friendless—The tree of knowledge—A child's prayers and doubts—Cause of the cruelty—A strange landscape—A halt—Journey continued—The castle

CONTENTS

xi

PAGES

couch—Scotch lad and English lady in Arab life—Night journeys and day halts—New clothes--No deliverance—Drogheda reached—At home on the Boyne—Sources of the narrative—Hugh Brontë's dramatic eloquence contrasted with that of his granddaughters—No traces of the journey—Searching for the Brontë house in vain.

CHAPTER VII.

A MISERABLE HOME .   .   .   .   .   51—66

A cold welcome—Settling conditions—Gallagher approves—The Blessed Virgin and saints introduced—An old grievance—Meg and her business—Destruction of bastards — Joseph in *Wuthering Heights* typed by Gallagher—Heathcliffe and Welsh—New company—Description of the mansion—Hugh's illness—Friendship with Keeper—Something to live for—Cocks—Aunt Mary kind—Tells him the Brontë tragedy—Returning spring and health—Keeper at work—Emily Brontë's Keeper—Irish home love—Awaiting his deliverer—Outgrowing his clothes—Growing to his surroundings—Hard slavery —The spy—The devil.

CHAPTER VIII.

THE CAPTIVE ESCAPES .   .   .   .   .   67—75

Welsh's quarrels—A bit of bog—Land agent—An agrarian battle—Welsh worsted—Hugh joins the enemy —Second battle of the Boyne and its results—Words of truth and deferred claims—Chaff bed and rival heir—Promised chastisement—A resourceful ally—Presentiment—Hugh trounces Gallagher—Final leave-taking—Kisses Keeper and plunges into the Boyne—A swim for life—Helped on his second great journey.

CHAPTER IX.

THE FLIGHT AND REFUGE .   .   .   .   76—78

On solid ground—The fugitive passes through Dunleer, Castlebellingham, and Dundalk—Turns eastward

xii   *CONTENTS*

PAGES

towards Carlingford—Finds work at Mount Pleasant
Kilns—Burning lime—New clothes—Free labour-·
Makes a new friend.

CHAPTER X.

LOVE AT FIRST SIGHT .   .   .   .   . 79—82

Visit to County Down—A surprise in store—An Irish
eauty—Alice McClory described—Hugh's discomfiture
—The Protestant bar—Hugh's eagerness—Alice cold.

CHAPTER XI.

TRUE LOVE AND PARTY STRIFE   .   .   . 83—91

Christmas holidays — Engagement — The Catholics
roused—Religious tests—The dying Orangeman—Perio-
dical party battles—12th of July and 17th of March—
Weapons—The great religious agitation—An Irish priest
—Alice and the priest—Hugh innocent of religion—Attempt to disarm prejudice—A conference ends in a fight
—*Contrairyness*—A dreadful speech—Hugh among the
Philistines—Saved by Alice—Tender good-bye—Hugh's
sudden conversion—The deepening of true love.

CHAPTER XIᵗ.

LOVE'S SUBTERFUGES   .   .   .   .   . 92—105

Burning lime—Hugh's inattention—Visits Alice—
Secret meetings—The Courting Bower—Traitors—A rival
lover produced—Hugh begins his education—A plot—
Dismissal—Hired to James Harshaw as a farm labourer
—The Harshaws' kind treatment—Hugh's duties—
Taught by the children—Hugh's doctrines—The Martins
—Jane Harshaw became the mother of John Martin, M.P.
—Martin meets Mitchell—Both transported—John Martin
and Hugh Brontë's doctrines—Palmerston and Martin
—Brontë lost sight of—Alice takes horse exercise—
Communicates with Hugh—Burns the rival—Marriage
arranged—Preparations—Wedding party arrived—Alice

CONTENTS

xiii

PAGES

elopes with Hugh—Married in Magherally Church—
Burns and the wedding party drink her health—The
fugitives forgiven.

CHAPTER XIII.

LOVE IN A COTTAGE . . . . . 106—113

At home with Red Paddy—The cottage in Emdale—
Present condition of the cottage—Rev. Patrick Brontë's
birthplace—The corn-kiln—17th of March, 1777—Emdale
and Haworth—Happy home—Honest poverty—Removal to a larger house—Increasing family—Parish
register—Hugh's verses on Alice.

CHAPTER XIV.

THE DAILY ROUND . . . . . 114—128

Beeking the kiln—A primitive kiln—Payment in kind
—Alice's spinning-wheel—Brontës clad in home-spun
—Brontë independence — Brontë a ditcher — Brontë
prosperity—MacAdam's discovery—Invention worked by
the Brontës—Farming and road-making—A public-house
—Turn of the tide—Decadence—Drinking habits—Rev.
D. McKee begins the temperance cause—The sermon
on the Rechabites—Dr. Edgar reads *The Rechabites*—
Empties his whiskey down the gutter—The temperance
crusade.

CHAPTER XV.

THE IRISH RACONTEUR, OR STORY-TELLER 129—141

The *hakkawāti*—His manner—His success—The
Irish *hakkawāti*—His hearers—Baby Patrick Brontë—
Hugh Brontë a moral teacher—His studies; his books
—His superstitions—Patrick inherited his father's gifts
—Emily Brontë and her father's stories—Miss Nussey's
testimony—Swinburne's insight — Emily's models—
Wuthering Heights thoroughly Brontë—Emily's art—
Brontë attributes.

xiv CONTENTS

CHAPTER XVI.

PAGES

HUGH BRONTË AS A TENANT-RIGHTER . 142—155

Lecture Bible in hand—Bible and Church—Protestant parsons—Catholic priests—Kings and emperors—King George III.—Landlords—The peasants—Law-making—Land agents and attorneys—The Brontë estate—Landlord art—Irish law and justice—Obedience—Patriotism—His animus—Battle of Ballynahinch—Hugh's escape—"Every man his own"—The cure for turbulence—Sharman Crawford's tenant-right—Crawford's views—Councillor Dodd—Cruelty to a child and the result.

CHAPTER XVII.

THE BRONTË FAMILY : GENEALOGICAL . 156—162

Summary—Defective records of Drumballyroney—Brontë baptismal register—The Brontë girls—Rev. John McCracken's testimony.

CHAPTER XVIII.

THE BRONTËS AL FRESCO . . . 163—174

McAllister's story—Six Brontë brothers—Ball-rolling—Curious phraseology—Odd appearance—Harvesting—Local report—The concert in the Glen—Sisters spinning and dancing—Brothers fiddling and dancing in turns—The scene—The spectators—Awe of the Brontës—Unsocial.

CHAPTER XIX.

THE BRONTËS, THE DEVIL, AND THE POTATO
BLIGHT . . . . . . 175—184

The potato blight—Different kinds of farmers and farming—Housekeeping—The lazy poor—Brontë industry—Brontë prosperity—Good landlord—Brontë

CONTENTS

xv

PAGES

paradise blasted—Theories—Common belief that the devil blighted the potatoes—Vivid recollections—Hugh Brontë's challenge—Offering to the fiend—Dramatic power.

CHAPTER XX.

MINOR AMUSEMENTS OF THE BRONTËS . 185—192

Want of a common holiday—Party days—Consumption of whiskey—Kind of drink—Fiery potations and orations—Party fights—Party balls—Christmas and New Year's Day—Easter Sunday and eggs—Shooting matches—Cock-fighting—Patrick as a marksman and sportsman—Wakes and funerals—Boxing—Incident in Rathfriland fair—Gathering may-flowers.

CHAPTER XXI.

THE GREAT BRONTË BATTLE . . . 193—204

The local Hĕjĭra—The fight between Sam Clarke and Welsh Brontë—Origin of the battle—Peggy Campbell — The schoolboys' cruelty — Welsh intervenes—Ducking the cripple—The duckers ducked—The challenge—The preparations—The crowd—Public opinion—Clarke's mother—Welsh's sweetheart—Spartan speech —Long endurance—Final command—Crushing victory—Peaceful result —Traditions—Welsh's repentance.

CHAPTER XXII.

THE BRONTËS AND THE GHOSTS . . 205—218

The haunted Glen—A tragedy—Brontë habits—The suicide — The headless man — Ghost-baiting — Hugh Brontë with sword and Bible—Contest in the mill—Strange surmises—The wailing child—The black horse —Grinning skull—Apparitions in Frazer's house—Chal-

xvi CONTENTS

PAGES

lenging the ghost—Tne ghost's squeeze and Hugh's death—Hugh Norton's account—The headless horseman —Minute description—Kaly Nesbit's account—A naggin of whiskey—Captain Mayne Reid—His Texan tale— Reception in Ballynaskeagh—A practical age.

CHAPTER XXIII.

PATRICK BRONTË'S CHILDHOOD AND EARLY SUR-
ROUNDINGS . . . . . 219—228

Birth—Name—Early experiences—Fed on stories— Poverty—Simple living—Different kinds of bread— Sowans—Luxuries and dainties—Tea—Young Bron'ë's occupation — His clothes—"Pat the Papish"—Tormented by Protestant lads—Blacksmith's shop—Apprenticed to weaving—Cultivation of flax—His sisters span —The prosperous weaver—Book hunger.

CHAPTER XXIV.

PATRICK BRONTË'S SCHOOLS AND SCHOOL-
MASTERS . . . . . 229—237

A divided mind—Milton's attractions—A friend in need—The "Stickit Minister"—Education of ministers —Patrick and Harshaw—Laying plans—Brontë's education—Lights—Weaving and learning—Incessant application—overcomir g obstacles.

CHAPTER XXV.

LEARNING AND TEACHING . . . 238—253

The loom abandoned—Rival candidates for Glascar school—Appointed teacher to a Presbyterian school— Precentor—Attitude of the Orangemen—Sensible system —Whipping days—Gumption in school—Success in teaching—Night-school—Amusements—English litera-

CONTENTS xvii

PAGES

ture—The avenues of education—The Episcopal and Presbyterian ministers—Harshaw's guidance—Brontë's attainments—His reading—Books—Recreations—Observations—Adventure on Mourne Mountains—Skating —Patrick a poet—The poetry—The Vision of Hell— The characteristic pieces kept back—Palmerston and Devonshire—A love affair—A kiss and a quarrel— Dismissed from school—Harshaw's reproofs—Clandestine meetings—Helen faithless—Harshaw introduces him to Rector Tighe.

CHAPTER XXVI.

PATRICK BRONTË IN AN EPISCOPALIAN SCHOOL 259—261

Success in school—Private tuition—Few incidents— The Rev. Thomas Tighe—The vicar—Minutes of vestry.

CHAPTER XXVII.

PATRICK BRONTË AT ST. JOHN'S, CAMBRIDGE 262—267

Rector Tighe's help—Harshaw still his friend—Patrick Bronte matriculates — Hare Exhibition — Duchess of Suffolk Exhibitions—Goodman Exhibition—Remembering his mother—Coaching at Cambridge—Tutor and colleagues—Signature.

CHAPTER XXVIII.

THE IRISH BRONTËS AND "JANE EYRE" . 268—274

The novels first read in the Ballynaskeagh manse— Conflicting evidence—Patrick's letter to Hugh—The price paid for Charlotte's three novels—First editions in Ireland—Author's copies—The novels alarmed the uncles and aunts—Books shown to Mr. McKee, who admired them—Uncles pleased—Scene in the manse— McKee's verdict.

xviii   *CONTENTS*

CHAPTER XXIX.

PAGES

THE AVENGER IN SEARCH OF THE REVIEWER 275—292

Joy of the Irish uncles and aunts—Mr. McCracken's testimony—Mr. McKee's evidence—Favourable reviews of *Jane Eyre*—Public impression—The *Times*—The *Edinburgh Review—Blackwood's Magazine—Frazer's Magazine—Tait's Magazine*—Incense to the Brontës—The *Quarterly Review*—Effect in Ireland of the attack—McKee as comforter—The angry uncles—Hugh's vow—Preparing a shillelagh—Pickle and polish—Hugh starts for England—Arrives at Haworth on Sunday—Niece's curiosity—Hugh disappointed with his nieces—Branwell—Prize-fight—Robin Hood's helmet at Sir W. Armitage's—Hugh leaves Haworth for London—In lodgings—At John Murray's—Saw the editor of the *Review*—Reviewer tried to find out who Currer Bell was—Ceased to admit Hugh at Murray's—Hugh with the publishers—A friend at the British Museum—A private dinner—Promised assistance in searching for the reviewer—Hugh's resources—Opinions of booksellers—London explored—Return to Haworth—The vicarage gloomed—Anne's comfort and parting—A walk with Charlotte—Final parting—The mission a failure.

CHAPTER XXX.

WHO WROTE THE REVIEW? A WORKING HYPO-
THESIS   .   .   .   .   .   .   293—308

The unsolved question—The secret safe in the house of Murray—General detestation of the reviewer—Mrs. Gaskell's opinion—Swinburne's attack—Augustine Birrell's onslaught—Interpolation in the review—Vanity Fair—Becky disposed of, and Thackeray lauded—The reviewer grows moral—Specimen of the pagan and pharisaic patchwork—Difference in style and sentiment—Evidence of sentiment strongest—Reviewer guilty of what he condemns—Andrew Lang's views.

LIST OF ILLUSTRATIONS.

	PAGE
Patrick Brontë's Birthplace	*Frontispiece*
General View of Brontë Neighbourhood	xx
Ballynaskeagh Manse, where the Novels were first read	11
The Courting Bower	93
Map of the Brontë District	107
The Brontë Home	121
Plan of the Brontë Homeland	123
The Last of the Brontës' Aunts	157
Patrick Brontë	159
Charlotte Brontë	161
The Brontë Dancing Green	169
The Ducking Pond	195
The Haunted Glen	211
Glascar School, where Patrick Brontë first taught	239
Presbyterian Meeting House, where Patrick Brontë was Precentor	255
Patrick Brontë's Matriculation Signature	263
Patrick Brontë's Signature on proceeding to his Degree	266
Patrick to Hugh regarding the price paid for the Novels	269

GENERAL VIEW OF BRONTË NEIGHBOURHOOD.
Knock. Brontë House. Mourne Mountains. P. Brontë's Birthplace.

CHAPTER I

THE HIDDEN SOURCES

THE history of the Brontës resembles in a small way the history of the Nile. The great river was persistently explored, and minutely described in its meanderings through the fertile delta, and as far up, by pyramid and temple and tomb, as the explorers could go. Traveller followed traveller, each noting the discoveries of his predecessor and adding a few of his own; but until recent years the head secret of the great African river remained shrouded in impenetrable mystery. Many guesses were hazarded as to the Egyptian phenomenon, but the muddy river continued to ebb and flow, bearing its yearly burden of fertility to Egypt no one knowing whence. Thanks to modern investigation, we now know that the mysterious Nile is the natural outcome of vast lakes and other natural sources above. Explorers have seen, and we know.

The current of Brontë life and thought has been faithfully traced and minutely portrayed in its lower reaches through the fertile delta of England, but the higher reaches in Ireland have not been explored, and the head source has not been disclosed. The sources of information regarding the Brontës within the English area have been studiously investigated, and everything known regarding that singular family has been described with great wealth of literary skill and ingenuity ; but the explorers stopped short by the English boundaries, and the eager guesses and surmises as to what lay beyond have been nearly all wrong.

The Brontë phenomenon has always had fascinating attractions for the generous, the chivalrous, the unselfish ; but the heart of the mystery could no more be reached by investigating its English surroundings than the secrets of the Nile could be unravelled by the study of its muddy banks in Egypt.

Mrs. Gaskell's *Life of Charlotte Brontë* is an exquisite tribute from a gifted hand laid on a sister's grave ; but Mrs. Gaskell's dreary moorlands and dismal surroundings are as inadequate to account for the Brontë genius as the general picture of suppressed sadness is unwarranted by the Brontë letters taken as a whole, or by the living testimony of Miss Ellen Nussey, Charlotte's lifelong friend. Genius of the Brontë kind would not be so rare if grey and sombre surroundings

THE HIDDEN SOURCES

could produce it, or if it could be stimulated by chilling repression and cramped circumstances. The Gaskell biography, however, roused curiosity as well as sympathy ; and while the reader felt keenly for the desolate girls in the Yorkshire vicarage, he also felt that the whole story had not been told : hence the number of attempts by many hands to complete a biography which all felt to be only a fragment.

Mr. Wemyss Reid has given us a picture of the Brontës in brighter and truer colours, taken from the very same material in which Mrs. Gaskell found her sombre tints ; but Mr. Wemyss Reid's theory as to the " disillusioning " of Charlotte at Brussels is a pure assumption, repudiated with indignation by Miss Nussey, Charlotte's confidante, unwarranted by the correspondence, and quite incapable of supporting the structure which Mr. Wemyss Reid would build upon it. If Charlotte's genius required a love-disaster to quicken it, how shall we account for the kindling of Emily's genius— especially as Emily's simple heart was never ruffled by a love affair, and as the author of *Wuthering Heights* is admitted to be the most Brontë of all the gifted family ? Or how did it happen that the gentle Anne was moved to tell the story of *Agnes Grey* ?

Mr. Wemyss Reid's story stops short on English soil, and leaves the reader with an anxious desire to know more.

The Brontë problem attracted Mr. Augustine Birrell, and his brilliant *Life of Charlotte Brontë* contains some additional facts gleaned in England. The sketch is full of humour and pathos, and deserves to be read if only for the generous indignation called forth by the *Quarterly* reviewer who sought to assassinate the reputation of the author of *Jane Eyre*. But Mr. Birrell's sarcasm with regard to the Irish Brontës loses point when he is found to be simply following the mistakes of his predecessors.

Similar excellencies and defects mark the numerous books which have been written on the Brontës. We want more than intense enthusiasm, painstaking investigation, high appreciation, with only a few guesses thrown in where facts are needed. The builders of the Brontë fame have done their best on an Egyptian model, but the bricks used have been wanting in the Irish straw that would have given them cohesion, and hence the various structures are lacking in the elements of stability and thoroughness.

This feeling of dissatisfaction was felt in some degree by the writers themselves, but by none more clearly expressed than by Mr. J. A. Erskine Stuart, the author of a most useful book, *The Brontë Country*. After tracing the Brontës in England and Ireland as far as their footsteps were known, Mr. Erskine Stuart adds :—

THE HIDDEN SOURCES

"For our own part, we desire a fuller biography of the family than has yet been written, and we trust, and are confident, that such will yet appear, and that there are many surprises yet in store for students of this Celtic circle."*

I now proceed, but not without misgivings, to justify the confidence expressed by Mr. Erskine Stuart, and to fulfil the prediction implied so far as regards the Brontës in Ireland.

* *The Brontë Country*, by J. A. Erskine Stuart (Longmans, Green & Co.), p. 192.

CHAPTER II

THE CHIEF SOURCES OF INFORMATION:
PRELIMINARY

I PROPOSE in the following pages to supply the Irish straws of Brontë history which I have been accumulating for more than a quarter of a century, and to lift the curtain that conceals the origin of the family and the source of their genius.

I have waited in hopes that some more skilful hand might undertake the task; but as no one else, since the death of Captain Mayne Reid, has the requisite information, the story of the Irish Brontës must be told by me, or remain untold.

I have had exceptional advantages for undertaking the task. When a child I came into contact with the Irish Brontës, and even then I was startled by their genius, before any literary work had made their name famous in England. My first nurse had lived within a quarter of a mile of their home, and had a rich store of wild tales regarding them.

THE CHIEF SOURCES OF INFORMATION

My first classical teacher was the Rev. William McAllister of Finard, near Newry. As a child he had known Patrick Brontë, and he had often heard his father Hugh, the grandfather of Charlotte, narrate to a spellbound audience the incidents which formed the groundwork of *Wuthering Heights*. Mr. McAllister was a good teacher, though he taught me more of Brontë lore than of classic minutiæ. He aimed more at interesting his pupils in the story of Troy than at grounding them in the niceties of Greek grammar ; for he held that classics should be taught with the simple view of making the learner more proficient in the use of his own language.

He declared classical learning to be useful only in so far as it enriched the mind with new thoughts, and gave a larger wealth of vocabulary to the tongue. He taught me to reproduce the classic stories in English rather than to make translations ; and sometimes he would give me the plot of such works as the *Hecuba* or the *Alcestis*, and leave me to fill in the wording in my own way. In accordance with his theory, he often varied my task by giving me one of Hugh Brontë's stories to reproduce.

He used to take me for long walks through the fields, and tell me the story of Hugh Brontë's early life, or some of his other stories, which he assured me were just as striking and as worthy to be recounted as the wrath of Achilles or the wanderings of Pius Æneas. These stories I would reproduce, some-

8 THE BRONTËS IN IRELAND

times in writing, but oftener *vivâ voce*, with as much spirit as possible, dulness being the one quality that my tutor would not tolerate.

It thus happened that I wrote screeds of the Brontë novels before a line of them had been penned at Haworth ; and I do not think Branwell Brontë meant to deceive when he spoke of writing *Wuthering Heights*, for the story in outline must have been common property at Haworth, as it was largely the story of Grandfather Brontë, and the children of the vicarage were all scribblers. However that may have been, I read the Brontë novels with the feeling that I had already known what was coming, and I was chiefly interested in the wording and skilful manipulation of details, for I had become acquainted with the incidents of old Brontë's career, as well as with most of his stories, real and imaginary.

My teacher's relatives lived quite close to the Brontës. They were freeholders and local gentry in a small way, and through them I was able to verify facts and incidents which had come to me somewhat distorted, and rather artistic, through the medium of my teacher's brilliant imagination. The pains then taken to have the facts in their right proportion and setting have fixed them indelibly on my mind.

Besides these there were two brothers, John and

THE CHIEF SOURCES OF INFORMATION 9

James Todd, with who ! was acquainted, who knew the Brontës, anc ere brimful of their doings.

At a later period I had still better opportunities for forming a sound judgment regarding the Irish Brontës. The pleasantest parts of my undergraduate holidays were spent at the manse of the Rev. David McKee of Ballynaskeagh. Mr. McKee was a great educationalist. He was the instructor and friend of several hundred students, whom he prepared for college. Many of these afterwards occupied prominent places in the Church and at the Bar, and one of them, Captain Mayne Reid, dedicated *The White Chief* to his old teacher.

Mr. McKee not only gave a sound education to his pupils, but he had the power of inspiring almost every one of them with something of his own high moral purpose and chivalric tone.

He was the author of several books, one of which led to the commencement in Ireland of the temperance movement, which afterwards spread to Scotland and England. It was a common saying of his pupils that, had he lived with more favourable surroundings, he would have enriched the world with thoughts as brilliant as Carlyle's, but without Carlyle's bile.

This great and noble man, who stood six feet four inches high, was the friend of the Brontës, who were his near neighbours. He recognised the

THE BRONTËS IN IRELAND

Brontë genius where others only saw what was wild and unconventional.

The Brontës came to Mr. McKee, as did all his neighbours, for help, sympathy, and guidance; and the first house in Ireland in which the Brontë novels were read was the Ballynaskeagh manse.

Mr. McKee's home was the centre of mental activity in that neighbourhood, and the early copies of the novels that came to the "Uncle Brontës" were cut, read, and criticised by Mr. McKee, and his criticisms were forwarded to the nieces in Haworth.

Great was the joy of the Brontë uncles and aunts when Mr. McKee's approval was given to the works of their nieces. The arrival of *Jane Eyre* was an event of some importance. It was brought to the manse by Hugh Brontë before any notice of it had appeared. He handed it over to the great man with a doubtful air (of which more hereafter), as if it were the evidence of a youthful indiscretion on the part of his niece Charlotte.

That novel was read *en famille*, and sober work was suspended till it was finished. When the last word was read and all rose to disperse, Mr. McKee said, " That is the greatest novel that has been written in my time; but it is Brontë all over, from beginning to end."

It thus happened that I had opportunities of becoming acquainted with the Brontës under the

BALLYNASKEAGH MANSE, WHERE THE NOVELS WERE FIRST READ.

THE CHIEF SOURCES OF INFORMATION 13

most favourable circumstances. Besides these, several others who knew the Brontës, some of them still living, have kindly communicated to me the information they possessed, so that I have had side lights from many points on the many-sided Brontë phenomenon.

I have thought it right to give these personal details in this place, not only to show the qualifications I have for undertaking the story of the Brontës in Ireland, but more especially that I may not be obliged to interrupt my narrative by quoting authorities as I proceed, or by explaining how I came by my information.

I have spared no pains to make my narrative as complete as possible, although several characteristic stories will have to be omitted.

During my undergraduate days I once spent a couple of months in the south of Ireland dressed as a peasant, trying to trace some of the Brontë traditions to their sources. I have since made long journeys with a view to reconciling points that were at variance, and even during late years I have gone many times to Ireland to clear up, if possible, small matters that did not seem consistent with the main facts. I do not even now pretend to have reached absolute accuracy on every point referred to in the following pages, but the statements are as close approximations to fact as they can be made by patient industry ; and as I cannot hope for fresh light on matters still obscure, I do not see that anything would be gained by further delay.

I therefore submit this history of the Brontës in Ireland to the generous consideration of those who can discern that I have done my best with a difficult and complicated subject.

CHAPTER III

GRANDFATHER BRONTË'S EARLY HOME

HUGH BRONTË, the father of Patrick and grandfather of the famous novelists, first makes his appearance as if he had stepped out of a Brontë novel. His early experiences qualified him to take a permanent place beside the child Jane Eyre at Mrs. Reed's. The treatment that embittered his childhood is never referred to by the granddaughters in their correspondence ; but it is quite evident that the knowledge of his hardships dominated their minds and gave a bent to their imaginations when depicting the misery of young lives dependent on charity.

Story-telling, as we shall see, was a hereditary gift in the Brontë family, and Patrick inherited it from his father. Charlotte's friend, Miss Ellen Nussey, has often told me of the marvellous fascination with which the girls would hang on their father's lips as he depicted scene after scene of some tragic story in glowing words and with harrowing details. The breakfast would remain untouched till the story had passed the crisis, and sometimes the narration became so real and vivid and intense that the listeners begged the vicar to proceed no farther. Sleepless nights succeeded story-telling evenings at the vicarage.

Hugh Brontë, according to his own account, belonged to a large family of brothers and sisters. His father lived somewhere in the south of Ireland. He was a man in prosperous circumstances, and Hugh's early childhood was spent in a comfortable home.

Some time about the middle of last century, or a little earlier, the family was thrown into excitement by the arrival of an uncle and aunt of whom they had never heard.

The children at first thought the new-comers very rude and common, and they did not like the uncle's swarthy complexion and dark glancing eyes; but as they remained guests for a considerable time, first impressions wore off.

Hugh believed he was then about five or six years old. He soon became a great favourite with the new-comers, who took him with them wherever they went and had him to sleep with them at night. The child was their constant companion. They bought him little things that pleased him, and when they had completely won his heart they proposed to him that, as they had no children of their own, he should go home with them and be their son.

GRANDFATHER BRONTE'S EARLY HOME   17

Hugh believed, in later life, that the whole matter had already been arranged between his father and uncle, but that the uncle was allowed time to overcome the bad impression produced by his sinister looks, and to carry out the matter in his own way. This he did by holding out visions of ponies, and carriages, and dogs, and guns, and fishing-rods, until the child's imagination was on fire, and he pleaded with his father to let him go with his uncle.

Consent was given, and paradise, unguarded by cherubim or flaming sword, lay open before the child. He longed for the day when he might begin to spend his life among ponies and dogs, and ramble through orchards and among flowers, and fish for trout in the river Boyne, and be a great scholar (for that was part of the programme), with his good uncle and aunt approving, and his brothers and sisters coming often to see him in his glory and enjoy the fun. The day, or rather the night, came soon enough—a night to be remembered.

Many years later the old man, then *beeking* a corn-kiln in County Down, used to tell on winter nights the story of his early life, but he never failed to dwell on the simple incidents of that night.

He had waited with impatience the arrival of a local dressmaker, who brought him late at night a special suit of clothes to travel in. When the clothes were fitted on he was raised on a chair to give the dressmaker the *beverage* of them. The first kiss in new clothes in Ireland is a special favour. It is called "the beverage," and is supposed to confer good luck.

Hugh's sisters thronged round him for "second beverage," but the kiss and squeeze of the dressmaker remained a lifelong memory. He always believed that she had a presentiment of the fate that awaited him, for her voice choked and her eyes filled with tears as she turned away from him.

Standing on the chair he received the last adieux of his numerous brothers and sisters. His mother, who never seemed happy about his going away, but whose opposition was always borne down, did not appear for the parting farewell. For the previous few days she had been accustomed to take him into her lap, and with eyes full of tears heap endearing epithets upon him, such as "My sweet flower"; but he always broke away from her not being in a mood to appreciate sympathy.

His father lifted him in his arms and carried him out into the darkness, and placed him gently between his uncle and aunt on a seat with a raised back, which was laid across a cart from side to side. Sitting aloft on the cross-seat of the vehicle, the prototype of the Irish gig, little Hugh Brontë, with heart full of childish anticipations, began his rough journey out into the big world.

CHAPTER IV

THE FOUNDLING AND FOSTER-FRIENDS

WE must now leave little Hugh Brontë with his new friends until we have a fuller acquaintance with the uncle to whom he has been committed. Hugh Brontë's father, the great-great-grandfather of the novelists, used to live in a farm on the banks of the Boyne, somewhere above Drogheda. Besides being a farmer he was a cattle-dealer, and he often crossed from Drogheda to Liverpool to dispose of his cattle.

On one of his return journeys from Liverpool a strange child was found in a bundle in the hold of the vessel. It was very young, very black, very dirty, and almost without clothing of any kind. No one on board knew whence it had come, and no one seemed to care what became of it. There was no doctor in the ship, and no woman except Mrs. Brontë, who had accompanied her husband to Liverpool.

The child was thrown on the deck. Some one said, " Toss it overboard "; but no one would touch

THE BRONTËS IN IRELAND

it, and its cries were distressing. From sheer pity Mrs. Brontë was obliged to succour the abandoned infant.

On reaching Drogheda it was taken ashore for food and clothing, with the intention of sending it back to Liverpool; but the captain would not allow it to be brought aboard his ship again. There was no foundling hospital nearer than Dublin; and in those days Dublin was far from Drogheda. There was a vestry tax at that time for the carriage of illegitimate children to foundling hospitals, but as no one in Drogheda had an interest in the child being removed, it was left in Mrs. Brontë's hands, and she found it much easier to take it home than to carry it to Dublin, where it might possibly have been refused admission among the authorised foundlings. The Brontës even at that early period were of a golden hue, and they exceedingly disliked the swarthy infant; but "pity melts the heart to love," and Mrs. Brontë brought it up among her own children.

When the little foundling was carried up out of the hold of the vessel, it was supposed to be a Welsh child on account of its colour. It might doubtless have laid claim to a more Oriental descent, but when it became a member of the Brontë family they called it "Welsh."

Little Welsh was a weak, delicate, and fretful thing, and being despised for his colour and origin,

THE FOUNDLING AND FOSTER-FRIENDS 21

and generally pushed aside by the vigorous young Brontës, he grew up morose, envious, and cunning. He used secretly to break the toys, destroy the flower-beds, kill the birds, and stealthily play so many spiteful tricks on the children that he was continually receiving chastisement at their hands. For though they seldom caught him in the monkeyish acts of which he was accused, they attributed all the mischief to him, and detested and punished him accordingly. On his part he maintained a moody, sullen silence, only broken when Mr. Brontë was present to protect him.

He became a favourite with Mr. Brontë, partly because he was weak and needed his protection, and partly because he always came running to meet him on his return home, as if he were glad to see him and anxious to render him any assistance in his power. He followed his master about while at home with dog-like fidelity, and he generally managed to tell him everything he knew to the other children's disadvantage. He thus succeeded in securing a permanent place between the children and their father.

Old Brontë took Welsh with him to fairs and markets, instead of his own sons, as soon as he was able to go, and he found him of the greatest service. His very insignificance added to his usefulness. He would mingle with the people from whom Brontë wished to purchase cattle, find out from their conversation among themselves the lowest price they would be willing to take, and report to his master. Brontë would then go to the dealers, and without the usual weary process of bargaining offer them straight off a little less than he knew they wanted, and secure the cattle.

In Liverpool also Welsh would mingle with the buyers, who no more suspected his business than they suspected the street dog, and spoke freely what Welsh had come to hear. Brontë became a rich and prosperous dealer, and Welsh became indispensable to him, and followed him like his shadow by day, and at night was to be found coiled up beside him like his dog ; but the more Brontë became attached to Welsh the more his children despised and hated the interloper.

As time passed Brontë's affairs passed more and more into the hands of his assistant, until at last he had almost the entire management. They were returning from Liverpool after selling the largest drove of cattle that had ever crossed the Channel, when suddenly Brontë died on board. Welsh, who was with him at the time of his death, professed to know nothing of his master's money, and as all books and accounts had been made away with, no one could tell what had become of the cash received for the cattle.

The young Brontës, who were now almost men and women, had been brought up in comparative

THE FOUNDLING AND FOSTER-FRIENDS   23

luxury. Their wants had always been supplied
from their father's purse, they knew not how.
They were well educated, and had been a good
deal in England ; but they neither understood
farming nor dealing, and besides the capital
employed in dealing had been lost, and the land
so neglected that it was not in a condition to
support a family, even if the requisite capital and
skill for its cultivation had been forthcoming.

In this emergency Welsh requested an interview
with the brothers and sisters together. He declared
that he had a proposal to make that would restore
the fallen fortunes of the family. He had been
forbidden the house ; but as it was supposed he
was going to give back the money which he
must have stolen, his request was reluctantly
acceded to.

At the interview Welsh appeared dressed up as
he had never been seen before. He was arrayed
in broadcloth, black and shiny as his well-greased
hair, and in fine linen, white and glistening as
his prominent teeth. The upholstering must have
been costly, but the effect was ludicrous to those
who had known the man all their lives. The
sinister look was intensified by a smile of satisfaction that gave prominence at once to the cast
in both eyes and to the jackal-like dentals.

When all were assembled he began at once in
the grand cattle-dealer style to express sympathy

with the family, and to declare that on one condition he would carry on the dealing, and supply the wants of the family, as if nothing had happened. The condition was that the youngest sister, Mary, should become his wife. The proposal was rejected with a great outburst of indignant scorn. Many hot and bitter words were exchanged ; but as Welsh was leaving the house he turned and said, "Mary shall yet be my wife, and I will scatter the rest of you like chaff from this house, which shall be my home." With these words he passed out into the darkness.

The interview had two immediate results : it revealed to the brothers the dangers that threatened them, and roused them to an earnest effort to save their home. Welsh had shown his hand, and must be thwarted. He had robbed them, but he must not be permitted to ruin and disgrace them. That his cunning and malignity might be harmless the boys must bend their necks to the yoke of labour. They had many friends, and in a short time the three brothers were employed in remunerative occupations, two of them in England and one in Ireland. They were able to send home enough to pay the rent of the farm and to maintain their mother and sisters in comfort.

But Welsh was also roused to gain his end, and it was certain he would not scruple to use any means by which he might carry out his

THE FOUNDLING AND FOSTER-FRIENDS 25

purpose. He did not return to the cattle-dealing, for which by himself he knew he had no skill; but he soon found a post from which he hoped to avenge past indignities and gratify his greed and lust.

The landlord of Brontë's farm was an " absentee." The estate was administered by an agent. He was the great man of the district—local magistrate, grand juror, and pasha in general. His real business was the collection of rent, and for this purpose a parliament of landlords had given him despotic powers, absolute and irresponsible in matters of property, limb, and life. The agent was served by attorneys, bailiffs, and sub-agents, the Bashi-bazouks of those days. One of the offices of sub-agent was open, and Welsh was appointed to it in return for a large bribe paid to the agent.

The business of the sub-agent was to act as buffer between the tenant and the " squire," as the agent was always called. The sub-agent was generally a man without heart, conscience, or bowels, selected from the basest of the people. Like the genuine Bashi-bazouk, he had nominal wages, never paid and never demanded; but he was generally able to squeeze a good deal out of the tenants, first by alarming them, and then by promising to stand their friend with the " rapacious agent."

THE BRONTËS IN IRELAND

The sub-agent exaggerated his influence with the squire, before whom he cringed and grovelled ; but at the same time he was the chief medium through which the agent knew the condition of the tenants and their ability to pay their rent. One of his duties was to mix with the people in their festivities, when whiskey had opened their hearts and loosened their tongues, and discover if they had any hidden resources from which they might be able to pay an increased rent.

Welsh's former practices among cattle-dealers, as well as his natural disposition, gave him great advantages in carrying out to his agent's satisfaction this part of his duty. He was the very man for the post of sub-agent. He had lived by cunning and served with treachery, and in his new occupation he had great scope for serving himself as well as his master. He was a man of great importance when dealing with the tenants, and seldom saw them without letting drop the fatal word "eviction." He was ever arrogant to the poor on the estate, whom he could have served, and cringing to the rich, who could serve him. He was a born sub-agent, and circumstances had favoured his development.

But Welsh, while serving the squire, and recouping himself off the tenants for the bribe he had paid him, never for a moment forgot that he had sought the office of sub-agent for the double pur-

THE FOUNDLING AND FOSTER-FRIENDS 27

pose of getting hold of his late master's farm and with it the person of Mary Brontë. He at once drew the agent's attention to the derelict condition of the farm, and to the likelihood of the rent falling into arrears, and in the interest of the estate declared himself willing to undertake the burden of his late master's desolate homestead. He could not bear to see the family rudely evicted, or the place to pass into the occupation of strangers!

The agent promised that the farm should be transferred to Welsh on payment of a certain sum in case the Brontës were unable to pay the rent; but the rent did not fall into arrears. On the contrary, the agent's demands were regularly and punctually met, and besides considerable sums of money were spent in decorating the house and improving the land.

Welsh pointed out to the agent that the Brontës were earning good wages in England, and the rent was accordingly raised; but the increased rent was paid on the day it fell due, and again raised in consequence.

Welsh, finding himself foiled in his short cut to his master's homestead, and considering that in future he might have to pay the increased rent himself, resolved to change his tactics, and turn his attention to the other object of his quest, Mary Brontë.

In the neighbourhood there lived a female sub-agent called Meg, as base and unprincipled as himself. Her chief duty was the secret removal of illegitimate children to the foundling hospital in Dublin. Her services were utilised in many ways. She was useful in conveying bottles of whiskey to farmers' wives who were getting into drinking habits, and in aiding farmers' sons and daughters to dispose of eggs and apples and meal purloined from their parents, in return for trinkets and ornaments which they wished to possess. She had also great skill in furthering the wicked designs of rich but immoral men. She was the *spey-woman*, who used to tell the fortunes of servant-girls and lure them to their destruction.

Like the male sub-agents, such women were generally supposed to possess the black art, and to have sold themselves to the devil.

Welsh employed this vile harpy to be his go-between with Mary. She was to say that he loved her to distraction ; that he was dying to speak to her ; that he was now passing rich, and in great favour with the landlord, who was likely soon to make him chief agent; that he would be local magistrate, grand juror, and, in fact, magnate and squire of the district. In support of these forecasts Welsh used to drive past the Brontës' house in a carriage borrowed for the occasion from a gentleman-farmer whose rent was in arrears.

The *spey-woman* came often to tell the servants'

THE FOUNDLING AND FOSTER-FRIENDS

fortunes, and she had many opportunities of telling Mary of Welsh's love and goodness. She told how for several years he had restrained the agent by his entreaties from evicting them from their home, and that he had yearly paid large sums to the agent to prevent him from carrying out his designs. All this seemed incredible to the simple-minded girl, but the harpy was able to show the receipts for the money on the same official form in which they were accustomed to receive the receipts for their rent.

After a time Mary listened to the vile woman's tales. Welsh could not be so bad as they believed him to be! Flowers taken from the gardens of tenants found their way in great profusion to Mary's room. Trinkets wrung from anguish-stricken tenants in fear of eviction were laid on Mary's dressing-table, for the servants had been drawn into the conspiracy. At length Mary agreed to meet Welsh in a lone plantation on the farm, in company with the harpy, that she might express to him her gratitude for protecting the dear old home. That meeting sealed Mary's fate. She felt she could never again look any decent man in the face, so she consented to marry Welsh to cover her shame. The marriage was secretly performed by one of the *buckle-beggars* of the time, and then publicly proclaimed. Welsh was now the husband of one of the ladies on the farm, and

30 THE BRONTËS IN IRELAND

for a substantial fine the agent accepted him as tenant.

The brothers, on hearing the news, which travelled slowly in those days, hurried back to the old home, but arrived too late.

The agent received them with great courtesy. They reminded him that their ancestors had reclaimed the place from mere bog and wilderness ; that their father had expended several thousand pounds on building the houses and draining the land ; that even within the last few years they themselves had expended large sums on the place, and had submitted to several raisings of the rent without demur ; and that now their old home with all these improvements had been confiscated without cause or notice, and handed over to the man who had robbed and degraded the family.

The agent seemed greatly pained. He was very sorry for the family, but of course he was only an agent, and obliged to do whatever the landlord desired, however unreasonable he might in his private capacity consider the landlord's views. Everybody knew that the landlord was a resolute man, and he could hold out no hope of being able to prevail on him to change his determination. Failing to get redress from the agent, the brothers unfortunately took the law into their own hands, and were arrested for trespass and assault. They were tried before the agent, who, with unruffled

THE FOUNDLING AND FOSTER-FRIENDS 31

courtesy and sympathetic demeanour, sent them to prison and hard labour.

He spoke of the pain with which he was obliged to vindicate " law and order," and gently reproached them for their lack of gratitude to the chivalrous gentleman who had relieved them of the burden of a neglected farm and made it a home for their penniless sisters.

Thus the man Welsh, who afterwards assumed the name Brontë, carried out his purpose of possessing his late master's farm and with it the person of his youngest daughter.

His threat of vengeance was also carried out— mother, sisters, brothers were scattered abroad, and so effectively that I have not been able, after much searching, to find a single trace of them.

This sordid transaction, which was an ordinary affair in Ireland, was fraught with far-reaching consequences to landlordism. It gave birth to a tenant-right theory, of which we shall hear something in a subsequent chapter.

CHAPTER V

THE ADOPTION AND OATH

WE must now return to little Hugh Brontë, whom we last saw passing out into the darkness from his father's house, seated between his uncle and aunt. In Hugh's newly discovered relatives we recognise Welsh and Mary Brontë.

Many years had passed since the events recorded in the last chapter. The agent there referred to had fallen by the hand of an assassin after a bout of heartless evictions, and almost simultaneously the house from which the Brontës had been driven was burnt to the ground, and all Welsh's ill-gotten riches perished in the conflagration. He was left a poor and ruined man, unable to propitiate the newly appointed agent with a satisfactory bribe, and hence he had to relinquish the sub-agency so congenial to his tastes.

Welsh was always able to subordinate his pride to his interests, and through his wife he succeeded in opening correspondence with one of her brothers, a prosperous man settled in Ireland.

THE ADOPTION AND OATH 33

Welsh expressed deep penitence for all the wrongs he had inflicted on the family, and declared his earnest desire, if forgiven, to make amends.

He and Mary were then childless. They were getting on in years, and they professed to be troubled at the prospect of the farm, for lack of an heir, passing to strangers. They offered to adopt one of their numerous nephews, and to bring him up as their own son.

Conditions of adoption were agreed on, including such matters as education; but the chief item was a solemn oath, by which the father agreed never to visit or communicate with his son in any way, and Welsh and Mary Brontë bound themselves on their part never to let the child know where his father lived.

The family oath in Ireland was regarded with superstitious awe, and bound like destiny. Few of the peasantry ever considered official oaths in law courts binding. With them the formal kissing of the Book, at the command of a brusque and contemptuous official, had none of the sanctions of religion, superstition, or justice. The court oath had come to be recognised as simply a screw in the wheel of the oppressor. But the family covenant was a different instrument, and the man who broke it was perjured and abandoned beyond all hope of salvation here or hereafter. The infringement of the sacred oath shut for ever the gates of mercy.

34   *THE BRONTËS IN IRELAND*

The Brontë covenant was faithfully kept, and even when Mary visited Hugh in County Down, some time about the beginning of this century, she could neither be coaxed nor compelled to give him either directly or indirectly a clue or hint by which he might discover the home of his childhood.

It thus happened that Hugh Brontë was never able to retrace his steps to his father's house after the darkness closed around him, perched aloft on the cross-seat of a country cart between his uncle and aunt.

CHAPTER VI

A FEARFUL JOURNEY

IT was a cold night, and the child, coming from the bright and warm house, crept close under his aunt's wing for warmth. Soon the little full heart overflowed, and he began to prattle in his childish way, as he had done with his new friends for several days.

Suddenly a harsh torrent of corrosive words burst from Welsh, commanding him to stop gabbling and not to let another sound pass his lips. For a moment the child was stunned and bewildered. He had never heard any words escape his uncle's lips except words of kindness and approval, but the fierce stern violence of the angry order fell like a blow. The young Brontë blood could not, however, rest passively in such a crisis. Hugh, disentangling himself from his aunt's shawl, drew towards his uncle and said, " Did you speak those unkind words to me ? "

" I'll teach you to disobey me, you magnificent whelp ! " rasped out Welsh, and suiting the action

to the word brought his great hand down with a
sharp smack on the little fellow's face. Hurt
and angry, little Brontë sprang from the seat into
the bottom of the cart, and facing the cruel uncle
shouted, "I won't go with you one step farther!
I will go back and tell my father what a bad old
monster you are." And then, clutching at the reins,
he screamed, "Turn the horse round and take me
home!" He saw the lights of home shining out
warm into the darkness, but he felt a heavy hand
grasping him and choking the voice out of him.
Light flashed from his eyes, and he felt blood
flowing from his nose, and he was conscious that
he was being shaken and knocked against the
bottom and sides of the cart, and sworn at, and
that he was neither able to escape nor to speak.

Several hours later he woke up, and found himself lying in damp straw at the back end of the
cart, behind the seat on which his uncle and aunt
were riding. He felt sick and sore and hungry.
He had been dreaming that he was attacked by a
fierce, wild monster; but his father had come and
slain the monster and saved him, and he lay awake
listening for his father's footsteps and voice. He
waited long, but his father did not come. Every
jolt of the springless cart pained him, as there was
little straw between him and the bare boards.

It was a moonlight night, with occasional showers.
He watched the watery moon racing behind the

clouds, and the stars following in the same headlong career, sometimes hiding behind dark masses, and again shooting brightly and freely across open spaces. He had never seen the sky look so strange. He had always known things as friendly to him. He loved to look up at night, and he had always thought that the heavens smiled lovingly back on him ; but on that night he perceived that the cloud racks and careering stars were selfishly following their own courses and cared nothing for him.

He turned on his side and watched the two figures on the seat above him, riding along side by side in silence and caring nothing for him. A few hours before he had loved them with all the romantic and passionate love of his young heart. Now the whole current was changed, and he hated them to loathing. He felt the utter desolation of loneliness. His thoughts rushed home as he remembered the comforts and kindness he had left behind, and believed then, child though he was, that he had lost that home for ever. He had tasted the fruit of the tree of knowledge that night, and had grown in experience of good and evil.

That was the first night he ever remembered on which he had neglected to say his prayers. His mother had taught him to pray, and when he prayed he believed that God heard him and took care of him in the darkness. Was it because he had forgotten to say his prayers that God had left him alone with the unsympathising moon and stars, and with the cruel man and woman who had him at their mercy? He rose to his knees, put up his little folded hands, and said the prayer by which children come to their heavenly Father—the only prayer he knew.

When he came to the words, "Bless father and mother, and my good uncle and aunt," he felt the unsuitableness of his simple liturgy for his present need; "good uncle and aunt" stuck in his throat, and he could not proceed. He was seized with great terror lest he had spoiled his prayer, and he wondered what would come of it, if God did not hear it. While he was perplexed with this thought the black cloud of scepticism for the first time darkened his little mind and obscured his simple faith, and he feared that God would not hear him. And then the forlorn and desolate child slid a little lower on the down grade, and the awful doubt came to him, he knew not whence, that perhaps there was no God at all, and in his distress he sobbed out, "O God, if there be a God, let me die!"

The sobbing sound startled the uncle. He turned suddenly round, and with his whip struck the kneeling child and prostrated him. Little Hugh did not see the blow coming, and for an instant he thought God had answered his prayer and killed him; but the blow was followed by

A FEARFUL JOURNEY

a hurricane of oaths and threats which left no doubt that it came from his uncle.

The child was badly hurt. The weal raised by the whip burned like a cord of fire. He did not cry, however. The philosophy of patient, passive resistance grew up in him, and he would not let his bad uncle know that he was suffering from the blow.

Seventy years after that night Hugh Brontë used to tell the story with great vividness, dwelling on his own feelings in their sequence, and in repeating the narrative he scarcely ever forgot a sentence or varied a word. He would say, " I grew fast that night : I was Christian child, ardent lover, vindictive hater, enthusiast, misanthrope, sceptic, atheist, and philosopher in one cruel hour. Undeserved blows from a hand we once loved fall heavy, and lead to many thoughts."

The child's mind was filled with a great tumult of feelings. His atheism was merely a spasm of the heart, and as he lay on the straw he wondered if God would let him die, and then, like a true Brontë, he prayed that his life might be spared until he should be avenged on his inhuman uncle.

Then he was a child again. His mother's form rose up before him ; he remembered how he had prayed at her knee, and slept safely. He remembered also the sad eyes which she had bent upon him during the past few days, and the sweet and gentle manner in which she had caressed him, and, while his thoughts were thus occupied, he imagined that he was again safe on her lap, and slept.

When he awoke it was broad day. He lay perfectly still, and heard an altercation going on between Welsh and his wife about fifty pounds. He did not then fully understand the subject of the quarrel, but he learned afterwards that Welsh expected Mary to prevail on her brother to pay £50 per annum in return for Hugh's prospects and bringing up.

The bitter wrangle closed by Welsh declaring he would murder both his wife and nephew and throw them into the river. Long silence followed this announcement, and then they began to pass a bottle of whiskey between them. Noticing that Hugh was awake, they passed it to him and ordered him to drink. He was thirsty, and put the bottle to his lips, but could not drink ; he had never tasted whiskey before, and it burnt him. His uncle, in taking back the bottle from him, spoke savagely, but did not strike him.

After a while he sat up in the straw and looked over the sides of the cart. He was in a strange and unknown land. On the west rose a mountain abloom with heather. The rising sun shone upon it, and gave a golden tint to the ruby heath. On the east, bordered by the sea, stretched a level

A FEARFUL JOURNEY

41

plain composed of barren bog and rocky scrubland. The morning sky was perfectly unclouded, and the sun, which had just risen out of a blood-red sea, was touching with silver the dewy grass and wet stones and gossamer cobwebs on the bushes.

There was no sign of human being within sight. Crows flew overhead, wheat-ears on the rocks flashed their white-ringed tails, hawks poised in the air over their prey ; but the land was desolate, and even the track on which the cart jogged heavily along could scarcely be called a road. As the wheels jolted from hole to hole the child felt his whole frame shaken almost to pieces. He was hungry and cold and in pain, but he was glad that God did not take him at his word and let him die in the darkness. Then he remembered the loving home that was receding farther and farther from him, and having repeated the simple prayer that his mother had taught him to say every morning, the weary, home-sick child sobbed himself again to sleep.

When he awoke the sun was shining hot in his face. He was alone in the cart, out of which the horse had been taken. At first his alarm was great, as he found he had been deserted by the people from whom he longed to escape ; but he found his aunt's heavy shawl spread over him, and he knew that she could not be very far away.

The cart had been drawn up close to a little

THE BRONTËS IN IRELAND

thatched cottage, which comprised under the same roof a grocer's shop and a public-house. He saw a loaf in the window and some apples, and he tried to get out of the cart, but was unable to do so. A blacksmith, whose smithy stood on the other side of the road, seeing his fruitless efforts, came to him and lifted him down ; and just as he was beginning hurriedly to tell the blacksmith the story of his wrongs, his aunt, who had approached him from behind, caught his arm and led him gently into the cottage. He had there some potatoes and buttermilk, and slept on a settle bed by the kitchen fire till late in the afternoon. He had not been permitted to speak to any one, and no one had spoken to him.

He was still dreaming of home when he was roughly pulled off the bed and told to mount the cart again. Heavy imprecations fell on his aunt, who detained him a little to wash the blood-stains off his face and make him ready to continue the journey. A penny *bap* was put into his hand, and he was allowed to buy apples with the few pence that had been put by his brothers and sisters into the pockets of his new clothes as *hansel.* "It was ten years," said old Brontë, "before I fingered another penny that I could call my own."

The bright promise of the morning was not fulfilled. As the shades of evening began to gather the journey was continued in a drizzling rain. A

A FEARFUL JOURNEY

43

bottle of fresh straw had been added to the hard bed on which little Hugh was to spend the night. Adapting himself to his circumstances, he arranged the straw under the cross-seat on which his uncle and aunt sat, so as to be sheltered from the rain. Then, placing his heap of apples and the *bap* beside him, he settled down in comparative comfort for the night, so soon does the human animal accommodate itself to its surroundings.

On the coast of Syria I once arranged with a ragged, rascally-looking Arab for a row in his boat. My companion was a Scotch Hebrew professor. It was a balmy afternoon, and we enjoyed and protracted our outing. We talked a little to our Arab in Arabic, and much about him of a not very complimentary character in our own tongue. I happened to drop some sympathetic words regarding the poor wretch, and suddenly his tongue became loosed in broad Scotch, and he told us his story. It was very simple.

Twenty years before, the English ship on which he served as a lad had been wrecked at Alexandretta, on the northern coast of Syria. He swam ashore, lived among the people of the coast till he had become one of themselves, and at the time we met him he was the husband of a common Arab woman and the father of a dusky progeny. He was content with his squalid existence, and never again wished to see his native heather.

THE BRONTËS IN IRELAND

I knew a lady in the Syrian desert, the devoted wife of a petty Arabian sheikh. She drew her blood from the bluest strain in England. She had gone down to dinner in the Palace on the arm of Wellington, and had been considered the belle and beauty of the Court. She had been wife to an English Lord Chancellor, a great Governor-general of India, and had moved in the highest rank of the society of her time. But she was content and happy to endure the privations of Bedawi life, and isolation from civilising influences, for the society of a husband who was not very clean or kind.

Comparing small things with great, we need not wonder, then, when we see little Hugh Brontë arranging his straw divan, and settling down soberly beside his frugal repast. His couch was his castle for the time.

The night was long, the rain was incessant; the horse stumbled and splashed through the mud, and the harsh uncle varied the monotony by sometimes whipping the horse into a trot, and then swearing at it when it did trot. By ten o'clock the next morning a large village was reached; but Hugh Brontë in after-years was never able to identify it, nor have I been able to conjecture after much searching its probable position.

In the village there was an inn of considerable importance. The child was carried stiff and cold

A FEARFUL JOURNEY

from the cart to a little room in the inn, in which he was put to bed. No one but his aunt had been allowed to come near him. After placing some bread and milk beside him, she took away his clothes and locked the door of the little room.

In the afternoon she returned, bringing with her a suit of bottle-green corduroy with shining brass buttons. The clothes were much too large for him, and the trousers were so stiff that he could scarcely sit down. He was hurried into the corduroys, of which he hated the smell, and after having some more bread and milk the journey was resumed. He never again saw his own warm, woollen garments, which had been exchanged for the corduroys and a horsecloth. The horse-cover became his coverlet by night, and beneath it he slept more comfortably than before on his straw couch.

On the following morning at an early hour, while Hugh was still asleep, they reached another large town. As usual the cart was drawn up at an inn, where the travellers passed the day. During the day, while Welsh was out in the town and his aunt dozing by the fire, Hugh slipped quietly to the innkeeper, and tried to tell him the story of his wrongs; but the man could not comprehend what he said, and he could not understand what the man said owing to the brogue. The child's earnestness drew a little crowd round him, and he was just beginning to make himself understood,

46 *THE BRONTËS IN IRELAND*

when the uncle returned suddenly and whisked him off to the cart, where he was obliged to spend the long afternoon, until at nightfall they resumed their journey.

He heard angry words between his uncle and the innkeeper, but no deliverance came, and his heart once more sank within him. He passed another miserable night, and on the forenoon of the following day they arrived at Drogheda.

After a short pause at Drogheda, during which he was not permitted to descend from the cart or communicate with any stranger, the journey was resumed, and the party arrived at Welsh's home on the banks of the Boyne late in the afternoon.

Such is the story of Hugh Brontë's journey from his father's home to Welsh's. It was first told me by my old tutor, the Rev. William McAllister, and confirmed subsequently by several of his friends who were men of education and intelligence. I was careful to get the details of the different nights' march as fully as possible, in hopes that they might give some clue to the route. By four independent narrators the account was repeated to me. The narrations differed in certain details, but all were agreed on the main incidents as I have given them. I have omitted several striking incidents of the journey on which all four were not agreed. Even in details the narrators did not differ greatly, but all were at one as to the four nights

A FEARFUL JOURNEY

spent on the road, the villages and towns passed through, the appearance of the country on the first morning of the journey, and other leading facts.

I have given a mere outline of Hugh Brontë's thrilling tale, without any attempt to reproduce his style. The experience of the boy on that dreadful journey was told by the man with dramatic power and pent-up passion, such as never failed to hold his listeners spellbound.

Nothing was wanting to give colour and reality to Hugh Brontë's eloquence. He spoke of the stunted trees on the wind-swept mountains, and ghostly shadows on the moon-bleached plains. He described the desolate bogs on the waysides, and the interminable stretches of road leading over narrow bridges and through shallow fords ; and sometimes he would thrill his audience by a description of the heavens on fire with stars, or the autumn stricken into gold by the setting sun. He possessed the rare faculty of seeing as well as thinking what he was speaking of. He made his listeners see and feel as well as hear.

Mr. McAllister had heard most of the orators of his time, including O'Connell and Cooke and Chalmers, but no man ever touched or roused and thrilled him by the force of eloquence as old Hugh Brontë had done.

It may be questioned if any tale ever told by Hugh Brontë's granddaughters equalled those which he narrated in wealth of imagination, or picturesque eloquence, or intensity of human feeling, or vividness of colouring, or immediate effect. The grandfather had few of the cultured literary touches of the novelists, but he was generally the hero of his own romances, and narrated them with a rugged pathos and ferocious energy which went straight to the heart, but cannot be transferred to paper.

Welsh Brontë travelled by night partly for the sake of economy in saving the expenses of lodgings, but more especially that little Hugh should see no landmarks by which his footsteps might ever be guided home. In both respects he was thoroughly successful. He was able to doze all day long in public-houses without charge ; and Hugh, though he believed he had come from the south, never had the slightest idea as to where his father's house was located.

Do the incidents of the journey give us any clue by which to discover the region where Hugh Brontë's father lived ? The journey occupied four whole nights of an average of from thirteen to fifteen hours each. The rate of progress on the bad roads would not much exceed two and a quarter miles per hour, and the whole distance traversed might be fairly supposed to be somewhere about a hundred or a hundred and twenty miles.

A FEARFUL JOURNEY

With these facts in view I spent the two months of my undergraduate holidays in trying to find the early home of Hugh Brontë. I went about my work dressed in the ordinary clothes of an Irish peasant. I lived with the people, and enjoyed their hospitality and fun. Everybody was willing to aid me in my researches after a lost home and friends, but with every assistance I could find no trace or tradition of a Brontë family south of the Boyne. I did not then altogether abandon my quest, and I have since written hundreds of letters on the subject to correspondents in various parts of Ireland. But unless some document, now unknown to me, comes to light, the early home of Hugh Brontë will never be known.*

What is of more importance is the fact that the ancient home of the Brontës, where Hugh's grandfather—the great-great-great-grandfather of the novelists—lived, was on the north side of the river Boyne, between Oldbridge and Navan, not far from the spot where William of Orange won the famous battle of the Boyne.

Some thirty-five years ago the place where the Brontë house once stood was pointed out to me The potato blight and other calamities have been

* It is quite possible I may have been on the wrong track. Mr. McCracken assures me that Hugh Brontë spoke with a distinctly Scotch accent. His journey, after all, may have been from the north, and the child may have mistaken the waters of a lake for the sea.

THE BRONTËS IN IRELAND

steadily removing landmarks in Ireland, and I fear that the local tradition has now faded from the district.

In this there is nothing surprising or unusual. Few families in Ireland of the rank of the Brontës could trace their pedigree to the sixth or seventh generation.* That the ancestors of the Brontës lived on the banks of the Boyne six or seven generations back is beyond all doubt. Hugh's account of the place was precise and definite, and his daughter Alice distinctly remembered the aunt Mary, Welsh's widow, coming from the neighbourhood of Drogheda to visit Hugh and his family in County Down. Indeed, she referred to the fact, in a short interview in 1890 with the Rev. J. B. Lusk, when she was on her deathbed.

---

* With the exception of Alice, with whom I was in correspondence, directly and indirectly, up to her death, none of the Irish Brontës knew anything of the early history of the family. I visited most of them, and the vague information they had to communicate was merely an echo from the English biographies. Even Alice mixed up different events in a way sometimes that made it difficult to disentangle them.

CHAPTER VII

A MISERABLE HOME

HUGH BRONTË arrived at his uncle's house hungry, weary, and numbed with cold. He was also suffering acute pain from the incessant jolting of the springless cart in which he had lain, and from his uncle's blows and shakings. He was a little mite in stiff corduroys, of which he loathed the smell and touch; but he learned to be less fastidious.

On his arrival his uncle had a short conversation with him, with a view to a right understanding as to their future relations and duties.

Seizing his little nephew and ward firmly by the two shoulders, and looking fiercely in his face, Welsh informed him that his father was a mean and black-hearted scoundrel. Welsh, according to his own account, had agreed to make Hugh his heir, and give him the "education of a gentleman," and in consideration of these advantages Hugh's father had promised to pay Welsh a sum of £50; but the *spalpeen* and deceiver had only paid £5, and Hugh

THE BRONTËS IN IRELAND

would have to work for his bread and go without education. These grave decisions were emphasised by a series of very strong words, which Hugh always repeated, but which my reader does not care to hear. Are they not written in the records of *Wuthering Heights*?

There was present at this family interview a tall, gaunt, half-naked savage, called Gallagher, who seemed to know all about the matter under discussion, as he expressed audible approval of everything Welsh said, and when he had finished called on the Blessed Virgin and all the saints to *blast* Hugh's father and protect his uncle. Encouraged on these lines, he submitted for Hugh's consideration the utter absurdity of a boy with such a father hoping for happiness here or for heaven hereafter, especially as he would have all the blessed saints against him.

This sanctimonious individual was the steward of Welsh's house. He had been very useful to Welsh as a spy when he was sub-agent of the estate. He would mix with the lowest strata of the people at fairs and markets, make them drunk, and extract their secrets. He thus succeeded in sounding depths to which the sub-agent could not descend. He also frequented dances, wakes, and funerals; and as he had a great power of turning on the outward signs of sympathy and sorrow, he became Welsh's most valuable ally. In fact, he was indis-

A MISERABLE HOME

pensable to the office in the successful management of the estate.

Hugh's father had once denounced Gallagher as a spy at a public gathering, and he was ignominiously ejected, and in return Gallagher had supplied the evidence—false evidence—which led to the conviction and imprisonment of the three brothers. On the murder of the agent and burning of the Brontë house, Welsh and his spy fell together, and they continued to hold together as master and servant.

Gallagher had been of service to Welsh in other ways. He was the associate of Meg, and had aided her in the schemes which led to Mary Brontë becoming Welsh's wife. He was present with Meg as a witness in the plantation on that fatal night when Mary consented to wed Welsh. She was given to understand that if she refused her shame would be trumpeted all over the land by Meg and Gallagher on the following day.

Gallagher was a partner with Meg in the foundling business, and they had more effective ways of dealing with superfluous children than have yet been discovered by our modern baby farmers. The children were supposed to be carried to the Dublin Foundling Hospital ; but no questions were asked and no receipts given, and the guilty parents were only too well pleased that their offsprings should go " where the wicked cease from troubling."

54   THE BRONTËS IN IRELAND

Gallagher and Meg knew their employers well, and acted in accordance with their wishes. The two con.ederates were closely bound together by their trade secret and by the common danger of exposure ; for although those were the palmy days of landlord " law and order," it was always possible that some meddlesome magistrate might so far deflect the law from its primary purpose—the extraction of rent—as to bring it to bear on the wholesale murder of bastards. The thing feared came to pass, and Gallagher and Meg were transported ; but it came out in the evidence that Welsh, in the period of his prosperity, had so taken advantage of his opportunities, that he might have had a houseful of heirs but for the friendly intervention of Meg and Gallagher.

Gallagher was the original from whom Emily Brontë drew her portrait of Joseph in *Wuthering Heights*. He was one of Hugh Brontë's chief characters. On him he used to pour out the copious vials of Brontë satire, scorn, and hatred. Everybody who knew anything of Hugh Brontë's stories must have heard of Gallagher. In fact, the name became of common use in the neighbourhood of Ballynaskeagh as a nickname for objectionable persons, and I think it is so used still. At present I know a County Down family in London who often employ the sobriquet in jest, though with a basis of seriousness. To my

A MISERABLE HOME

55

mind it is just as certain that Joseph is the lineal descendant of Gallagher as that Heathcliffe is modelled on Welsh. In neither case is there room for reasonable doubt.

Joseph's hypocrisy is of the stern Protestant type, Gallagher's of the wily Catholic type. Joseph raked the Bible promises to himself, and left the threatenings to his enemies; Gallagher took "the Blessed Virgin and all the saints" into his service, and arrayed them against his foes. Visitations which were calamities to Gallagher and his friends were judgments on his enemies. Joseph, like Gallagher, used language of unfathomable and indefinite virulency, and in all respects he follows the outline of his prototype, but he is not the very image of the man.

In Emily Brontë's hands, Joseph, the English villain, is less selfish, less cunning, less criminal, less dastardly than the Irish. Joseph, the ideal creation, is not a lovable character, but he is less hateful than the real Gallagher. It was to the companionship of this inhuman monster that Welsh committed his little nephew and ward.

As soon as Welsh and Gallagher had left off speaking, Hugh looked round the mansion to which he had become presumptive heir. A happy pig with a large and happy family lay in one side of the room in which he stood. Smouldering ashes on a hearth, under a great open chimney, indicated that the house was a place of human habitation. A stack of peat was heaped up on the other side of the fire from that devoted to the mother-pig and her progeny. A broad, square bedstead stood in the end of the room farthest from the fire, raised about a foot from the ground. The damp, uneven, earthen floor was unswept. There were a few chairs upholstered with straw ropes, and on the backs of these a succession of hens took their places in turn, preliminary to a loftier flight to the cross-beams close up to the thatch. It was a low room, so they had not to make a great effort to reach their perches. A lean, long-backed, rough-haired, yellow dog stood by the boy's side smelling him, but in a neutral frame of mind, and showing no signs of welcome.

Hugh had heard the hard, rasping words regarding his father's treachery, and about his own duties and prospects; but he did not take in fully the situation, and he simply by way of reply said, " Are you going home soon?"

" You are at home now," replied his uncle. " This is the only home you shall ever know, and you are beholden to me for it. No airs here, my fine fellow! Your father was glad to be rid of you, and this is the gratitude you show me for taking you to be my heir. Get to bed out of my way, and I'll find you something to do in the morning to keep you from becoming too great for the position."

A MISERABLE HOME

But in the morning the child was unable to leave the hard, damp bed, in which he had lain down with loathing. He had been obliged to lie across the foot of the bed at his uncle and aunt's feet, but his slumbers were disturbed by the grunting pig, and squealing young, which seemed to keep up an incessant struggle and contest for choice places. There were also two cocks, nearly over his head, that had several bouts of crowing in rivalry during the night, the hens occasionally expressing approval.

The uncle rose early to let out the hens to find the early worm, and the great mother-pig to take an airing. He then dragged little Hugh out of bed, doubtless that he might get early into training for the coming responsibilities of heirship. But the child, unable to stand, tottered on to the floor. His uncle at first thought him shamming, but fierce imprecations could not exorcise fever and delirium, and for many weeks little Hugh lingered between life and death.

No doctor saw him, but he remembered his hair being cut off, and he did not forget the unfailing two-milk posset with which his aunt kept him supplied. He remained weak and unable to go out during the winter, but he made many friends.

The pig had been allowed to depart as soon as she was considered convalescent and competent to manage her large family. The rough dog had proved a warm friend—dogs were always steadfast friends to the Brontës. He used to lie across the bed, beside the child, all day long, licking his face and hands, and waiting with patient fidelity his restoration to health. At night he would lie on the bare ground by the bedside, but as soon as the elders had vacated the bed in the morning he would take the empty place beside his little friend.

The dog's delight seemed to know no bounds when the child began to get out of bed for a few hours daily. He would make various kinds of inarticulate sounds to express his pent-up feelings, and cut uncouth capers all round, sometimes rushing outside the house and barking furiously, as if to decoy the invalid beyond the threshold into the open air. Then he would sit with him, and lie with him on the sheepskin by the fire, and with dog-like constancy and affection watch every movement of his little hero.

And the child in return loved the great shaggy creature with all the strength of his little crushed heart. Hugh Brontë used to say that at first he passionately longed for death, that he might escape from his squalid surroundings and from his tormentors; but with his growing love for the dog he earnestly desired to live, and he believed that but for the dog he should have died.

He also came to long for the crowing of the cocks in the morning. There were two of them; one a

A MISERABLE HOME 59

bantam, and the other a great barn-door bird with flaming comb and splendid tufts of feathers like a guardsman's helmet. The great cock tried to thrill the lady hens by a voice that should have struck terror into the hearts of bantams ; but the bantam retorted by a little piping, *perliteful* crow, that seemed to deprecate the vulgarity of seeking popularity by loud and pompous ways.

In the long, weary days the fowls became his attached friends. He used to save a few crumbs from his own scanty allowance, and they would feed from his hands without hurting him. Better still, his aunt Mary during his illness conceived a great affection for him, and loved him as if he were her own child. When Welsh was not present she would let him have an egg, or a little fresh butter, from the *meskin* that was prepared for the market, or, what was much more prized, a cup of peppermint-tea, the forerunner of the universal beverage.

Over the peppermint-tea Aunt Mary became communicative, and then, and in after-years, she told him secretly the tragic story of the Brontë family. It brought him no immediate relief at first, but in after-years it was a great source of satisfaction to him to know that the cowardly and tyrannical uncle was no Brontë at all, and not even an Irishman.

On the subject of Welsh's nationality Hugh

THE BRONTËS IN IRELAND

Brontë's fiery patriotism was wont to appear. He would denounce the foreigner as the blighter of his life and the curse of his country. The denunciation of the foreign element was always productive of mixed sentiments in County Down, where a large proportion of the people were descendants of either English or Scotch settlers ; but Hugh Brontë's convictions seemed always to grow more decisive in the face of opposition, and from the crucible of contradiction his words flowed like red-hot lava. His aunt's husband had been a dastardly despot as well as a base-born bully, and he held that all foreigners were like him.

The spring came early that year, and with it health and vigour. Hugh revelled in the fresh air with his faithful dog Keeper. His aunt had told him of the burning of the old Brontë house. He saw the extensive ruins, and he kept away as much as possible from Welsh's inhabited hovel, which consisted simply of one of the large rooms with a roof thrown over the charred and crumbling walls. The squalor and wretchedness of the home into which so many things crept at night, compared with the ruins of the house in which his father had been brought up, made a lasting impression on Hugh's mind.

But he was not long left to such reflections. As soon as he was able to go he was sent to herd the cattle, which were housed at night in other ruined

A MISERABLE HOME

rooms of the burnt edifice. Hugh's duty was to prevent the cows and sheep from passing over a low fence from their pasture to growing corn on the other side of the fence.

The days were long, but he enjoyed them. Keeper was a famous ratter, and there was much for him to do in that line ; but in his laborious efforts to exterminate the rats he never forgot his higher duties, and he would stop in the heat and excitement of an ardent hunt to head off any of the cattle that seemed disposed to trespass on forbidden ground. Keeper sometimes rewarded his master by capturing a rabbit, and then there would be a feast for both boy and dog.

Emily Brontë's love for her dog, which was actually called " Keeper," was a weak platonic affair, a girlish whim or lingering family tradition, compared with the deep, strong tie of interest and affection that bound the desolate boy and friendless dog to one another. Keeper had at first scanned the newly arrived child with a critical eye, and as a kind of rival had given him a cold welcome ; but he had watched by him in sickness as only a dog could, and adapted himself to every mood of his returning strength and growing spirit, never becoming too buoyant or boisterous until his health was completely restored. It was an affection based on common interests and mutual esteem, and required no treaty or covenant to render it binding.

THE BRONTËS IN IRELAND

The dog for years never lost sight of his master. Absence was not needed to make the heart grow fonder. He lay close to him at night, dreaming of happy morrows, and awoke to joy in his master's love and fellowship.

When Keeper received a kick, as he often did, the child showed sullen resentment, at the risk of being treated in the same humane fashion himself; and when little Brontë was being scolded or beaten by Welsh or Gallagher, which was a matter of almost daily occurrence, the dog showed dangerous signs of springing at the throat of the common enemy.

In no land has attachment to home so firm a grip of the heart as in Ireland. Hugh Brontë was a mere child when he passed from the light of his father's home into the darkness of night and servitude; but his heart never ceased to ache for the home of his childhood, and the friends he had lost. He used to watch every well-dressed man that appeared on the road passing the farm, in hope that he might be his father and deliverer, but his hopes were always blighted, as the traveller passed by on his own errand. He often started at night in bed, believing that he had heard familiar voices at the door; but the voices were not repeated to his waking ears.

Year followed year in slow procession and ever-varying form. Now it passed clad in the virgin

A MISERABLE HOME

robes of spring, accompanied by the joyous min-
strelsy of birds ; now decked in the bridal array
of autumn, russet and gold, with yellow grain and
rosy apples ; and now it settled in the snowy
shroud of death. Each season had its charms
for the Brontë child. The silent awaking of spring,
the storm-bent trees roaring like a sea rushing
on the beach, the brattling thunder and blue skies,
the lashing hail and silent snow, seemed a part
of the boy shut out to their companionship. He
grew up in solitariness, and looked on the elements
as friends ; but his heart never ceased to yearn
for the lost friends of his old home.

His corduroy suit soon became too small, but
it was pieced and patched until the original had
all been supplanted. When his boots became
unwearable he was obliged to go barefooted.
There was no comb, and little soap, among the
domestic arrangements of his uncle's home ; but
the boy enjoyed his rough, free life, revelling in
unkempt and unwashed nature. His highest enjoyment was to be away with his dog, beyond the
espionage of Gallagher and the rasping blasphemy
of Welsh. But his idle days with Keeper among
the bees in the clover soon gave place to sterner
duties. He had to gather potatoes after the
diggers in sleet and rain, collect stones off the
fields in winter to drain bog-land, take his part
in all the drudgery of an ill-cultivated farm from

THE BRONTËS IN IRELAND

sunrise to sunset, and then thresh and winnow grain in the barn till near midnight.

He had grown too big to sleep across the bed at the feet of his uncle and aunt, and he had to lie on a sack of chaff in the half-roofed barn. His uncle hated him with a fierce and bitter hatred. In fact, he never saw his uncle's face but it was ugly with anger, or heard his voice except in accents of reproach ; and he had come to expect nothing else, for his uncle once told him he could never beat him when he did not deserve it, for like a goat he was always going to mischief or coming from it.

Hugh had no one but Gallagher to whom he could speak during his working hours, and he found the cunning malignity of Gallagher harder to endure than the harsh cruelty of his uncle. He always felt the eye and shadow of the spy upon him. The boy's clear instinct told him Gallagher was a bad man, but sometimes the pent-up heart would overflow, and the sealed lips babble to the one human being near him ; and then Gallagher would feign sympathy and extract from the boy all his secrets, even those that his aunt had communicated to him in confidence. He would also lead him on by the memory of cruel wrongs to give expression to the passionate resentment that slumbered in him.

When Gallagher had got all the secrets that

A MISERABLE HOME

were in the boy's heart he would denounce him
to his uncle, setting forth each item in the manner
that would best stir up his cruelty. Sometimes
Gallagher would mock and jeer at the rags and
destitute condition of the boy, and tell him that
all his evils came upon him from the blessed saints
and because of his father's sins, and he would
assure him that the devil would carry him away
from the barn some night, as he had often taken
bad men's sons.

Hugh was not much alarmed by day at the
prospect of satanic visitations, but he used to lie
awake at night in the utmost terror of the fiend.
He used to cover his head for fear of seeing him,
and when he slept he dreamt of being chased and
carried off by demons.

Owing to Gallagher's words the peaceful nights,
in which he used to forget his griefs, became more
dreaded by him than the day.

It is very probable that Hugh may have con-
veyed to his sons something of his own early vivid
conceptions of a personal devil, for, as we shall see,
one of them used to go forth to actual physical
conflict with the fiend.

Gallagher used to drive Hugh almost wild by
telling him stories of the beatings he had administered to his father when they were both boys, the
facts having been quite the other way ; and indeed
the cruelties practised on the boy were Gallagher's

base revenge for the whippings that Hugh's father used to administer to him.

Gallagher employed every means that his cunning and malignity could devise to render the boy's life miserable. He would purloin eggs, and break the farming tools, and maim the cattle, in order to have him beaten by his uncle. And he always managed to be present when Hugh was beaten, and he would on these occasions assure him that the punishment came to him from " the blessed saints."

CHAPTER VIII

THE CAPTIVE ESCAPES

THE uncle was an ill-tempered, ill-conditioned man in all transactions with strangers as well as in his domestic relations. In fairs and markets he had many quarrels, and often came home bearing marks of violence. He had a standing quarrel with a neighbour about a piece of exhausted bog.

Nothing in Ireland is supposed to test a man's honesty like a piece of waste land lying contiguous to his own land. " If a man escape with honour as a trustee, try him with a bit of bog," is an Irish proverb. The temptation had come in Welsh's way when he was a sub-agent with great facilities for helping himself at the expense of the tenants. He had robbed the Brontës of their farm,—why should he hesitate to add a slice of bog to it? Of course he had more land than he could cultivate, but his neighbour's bog was just needed to round off his ill-gotten possession.

The owner was known by the office as a foolish and objectionable tenant, who actually had the audacity to vote at elections contrary to the conscientious convictions of his landlord, and under the circumstances the agent would be easily prevailed upon to let Welsh have what he wanted. There was not likely to be any trouble over the matter, for the bog was of little use to anybody; all the turf had been removed, and only a swamp remained covered with star-grass, and tenanted by water-hens, coots, and snipe.

The agent offered to let Welsh have his neighbour's bog for a consideration. Welsh paid the sum, but the tenant, being a cantankerous person, did not fall in pleasantly with the arrangement. Difficulties of a magnitude out of all proportion to the insignificance of the matter were raised.

The plundering of the Brontës had been watched by the neighbours with sullen indignation, but when it became known that the objectionable sub-agent was about to lay hands on the property of another farmer the smouldering fire burst into conflagration. Attempts to transfer the bog were frustrated, and while matters were in this unsatisfactory condition the agent was murdered and Welsh's house was burned to the ground.

The ownership of the bog remained in that doubtful condition so profitable to those in authority. Welsh had lost his official position, and for years the new agent gave fair promises to both claimants and accepted presents from both. The landlord would of course decide the matter, but he was always in foreign parts, and could not be troubled with such a small detail till he returned to Ireland.

Meanwhile both paid rent for the bog and fought for the useless star-grass. Welsh was persistent in maintaining his claim to the coveted possession. He would wade into the swamp up to his waist to cut the sapless star-grass, and one day, after many hot words with the owner, blows ensued, and he was badly beaten.

He called on Hugh, who was then a large boy of fifteen, to help; but he called in vain, for Hugh had listened to a full and detailed account of his uncle's crimes before the battle began. He was accused to his teeth of murdering old Brontë for his money, and betraying his daughter in order to rob the family of their estate. The misery he had brought to many homes was clearly set forth,.and in Welsh's attempt to take possession of his neighbour's property Hugh believed that he was utterly in the wrong, and deserved the beating he received; besides, the neighbour (whose name has escaped me) had always treated Hugh kindly, and on several occasions had shared with him the collation of bread and milk that had been brought to him in the fields in the afternoon.

This battle led to important issues. The uncle was carried home, bruised and bleeding, by

Gallagher and Hugh and put to bed. On the following morning he sent for Hugh. In a choking passion he demanded why he had not helped him in the fight. Hugh replied that he considered his uncle was in the wrong, but that in any case it would have been unfair for him to have interfered.

The uncle stormed as usual, but was unable to get out of bed to chastise his nephew. Hugh now found an opportunity that he had long been waiting for to press deferred claims.

He reminded his uncle of the false promises he had made to his parents and himself when taking him from his home; of his failure to send him to school, or even to provide him with clothes to wear; and he reproached him with the fiendish manner in which he had always treated him. He ended his harangue by a fierce demand that he would let him return home, or else that he would provide him with clothes and send him to school.

Hugh, having found the use of his tongue in his uncle's presence, pleaded his case with a courage that surprised himself. He told his uncle that he was a false and cruel bully, and that he thoroughly deserved the beating at the hands of the man he had tried to rob; and then, carried away by his rising passion, he told him he knew he was not a true Brontë, but a gutter-monster who had stolen the name; he defiantly added that he hoped

THE CAPTIVE ESCAPES 71

before long to be able to avenge his ancestors for the desecration of their name by thrashing him himself.

Having delivered this speech, Hugh became conscious that another crisis in his life had arrived. Even the chaff bed in the half-roofed barn would cease to be for him. His uncle's house was no ionger childless. A son and heir had come on the scene a twelvemonth before, and Hugh knew he had nothing to expect but the same harsh treatment either in the present or the future. He could not even hope, in the event of his uncle's death, to inherit the old Brontë home and restore its fallen fortunes, for a legal heir had arrived and was well in possession. His uncle also had promised to punish him once for all as soon as he got well. A severe beating was his immediate prospect, for Welsh seldom failed in carrying out his evil promises.

In a few days the uncle was out of bed and able to move about, his head wrapped in bandages and his two eyes draped in mourning. As he grew stronger he fixed the day on which he would chastise his nephew. Hugh saw that the time had come for him to shift for himself. He first resolved to fight his uncle, but on consideration he concluded that even if he should be victorious, victory would only make his position in the house more un-endurable. Then he resolved on flight ; but where

THE BRONTËS IN IRELAND

could he fly? He would certainly be followed and brought back, and then his state with his uncle would be worse than ever.

Besides, he was almost naked, and the few rags that hung around him left his body visible at many points. He could not consult Gallagher in his emergency, for during the suspense he never ceased to keep him in mind of his coming chastisement, and to assure him that it was the will of the saints that he should suffer for his father's sins. Keeper was his sole friend, but to escape with Keeper would lead to certain discovery.

Hugh was now in a state of rebellion, and in his desperation he went to his uncle's enemy.

People in their death-and-life struggle for freedom do not scrutinise too closely the credentials of those willing to assist them.

Hugh's neutrality during the battle must have commended him to the enemy, who indeed owed him something for not joining in the fight at a critical moment, when by stone or stick he might have turned the fortune of war in his uncle's favour. He told his uncle's chastiser the full tale of his sorrows, and found him a sympathising and resourceful ally.

The day on which Hugh was to get his great beating arrived. Everybody except Gallagher awaited it in gloomy silence; even Keeper seemed to know what was coming. The uncle had pro-

THE CAPTIVE ESCAPES

73

vided himself with a stout hazel rod, which he playfully called "the tickler." Aunt Mary's eyes were, as usual, red with weeping.

Preparation was made deliberately, and the chastisement was to be administered when the cattle were brought home at midday. Hugh and Gallagher spent that morning weeding in a field of oats, in a remote corner of the farm. Hugh was silent; but Gallagher was loquacious and exasperating. He devoted the whole morning to jeers and taunts and mockery.

As the hour arrived for Hugh to go for the cows, Gallagher surpassed all his previous brutality by telling him that he had once been his mother's lover. He was proceeding to develop his false but cruel tale, when Hugh, stung to the quick, and blind with passion, sprang upon his mother's defamer like a tiger. There was a short, fierce struggle, and Hugh had his tormentor on the ground, and was beating his face into a jelly, while at the same time Keeper was engaged in tearing the ruffian's clothes into shreds.

Hugh's fury cooled when Gallagher no longer resisted, and throwing his *thistle-hooks* on the top of him as he lay prostrate in the corn, he walked into the house. He bade his aunt, who was baking bread, good-bye, kissed the baby, and then left to bring home the cattle to be milked.

Keeper, who had laid aside his melancholy in

THE BRONTËS IN IRELAND

the encounter with Gallagher, responded to his master's whistle, and ran round him in wide circles barking and gambolling as if to keep his spirits up. As Hugh turned to take a last look at the old Brontë house, he saw Gallagher approaching Welsh, who was waiting near the cowshed, evidently enjoying the pleasures of the imagination.

The cattle were grazing on the banks of the Boyne, near the spot where a wing of William's army crossed, on that era-making day, in 1690. Hugh proceeded to the river, and deliberately divested himself of his rags preparatory to a plunge, as was his wont. He laid his tattered garments in a heap, and told Keeper to lie down upon them Then, throwing himself down naked beside his faithful friend, he took him in his arms and kissed him again and again, and starting up with a sob he plunged headlong into the river.

The clothes were placed in a little hollow behind a ridge, from which Keeper could not see his master enter the water, or mark the direction in which he had gone.

Hugh swam swiftly down the river. It was a swim for life. The current soon carried him opposite the farm of his uncle's enemy, who awaited his approach in a clump of willows by the water's edge. He had brought with him an improvised suit of clothes to further the boy's escape. The pockets of the coat were stuffed with oat-bread,

THE CAPTIVE ESCAPES 75

and there were a few pence in the pockets of the
trousers. Hugh hurried on the garments, which
were much too large for him, and thrust his feet,
the first time for seven years, into a pair of boots,
and with a heart full of gratitude to his helper,
and a final squeeze of his hand, unaccompanied
by words from either, Hugh Brontë, about fifteen
years old, started on his race for life and freedom.

CHAPTER IX

THE FLIGHT AND REFUGE

WE have now reached more solid ground in the life of Hugh Brontë, and from this point onward his career, and that of his descendants, lie before us within well-defined geographical limits.

With glad heart and buoyant spirits Hugh sped forward on the road to Dunleer, which town he passed through without pausing, and continuing his flight struck straight for Castlebellingham. To his latest days he spoke of the intoxication of joy with which he almost flew along the road, a boot in either hand. He did not know where the road led to, or whither he was going; but he believed there was a city of refuge somewhere before, and his pace was quickened by the lurking fear that the avenger might be on his heels.

As he approached Castlebellingham he heard a jaunting-car coming after him. He hid behind the fence till it had passed. It was laden with policemen, but in the summer evening light he could see that his uncle was not on the car.

THE FLIGHT AND REFUGE 77

He reached Dundalk at an early hour, and after a short sleep in the shelter of a hayrick, continued his journey, not by the public road, for freedom was too sweet to run any risks of being overtaken, but eastward through level fields, along the shore, where now runs the Dundalk and Greenore Railway. In a small public-house he was able to spend his last copper on a little food, and then he started for Carlingford, which he heard of from the publican as an important town behind the mountain.

When he had wandered by the shore for a couple of hours, he saw smoke rising on his left, and he turned inland from the sea and came upon lime-kilns at a place called Mount Pleasant. These kilns came to be known as Swift McNeil's, and people went from great distances to purchase lime as well for agriculture as for building purposes.

When Hugh arrived at the kilns there were thirty or forty carts from Down, Armagh, and Louth waiting for their loads, and there were not enough hands employed to keep up the supply. Lime-stone had to be quarried and wheeled to the kilns, then broken, and thrown in at the top with layers of coal. After burning for a time, the lime was drawn out from the eye of the kiln into shallow barrels and emptied into carts, the price being so much per barrel.

Here Hugh Brontë found his first job, and regular remuneration for his free labour. In a short time he had earned enough money to provide himself with a complete suit of clothes, the first he had had since he was six years of age, and he had now reached sixteen. His wages more than sufficed for his wants, and he had a great deal to spare for personal adornment. Being steady and much better dressed than the other workers, he was advanced to the responsible position of overseer.

Hugh became a favourite with the people who came for lime, as well as with his employers. Among the most regular customers were the Todds and the McAllisters of Ballynaskeagh and Glascar in County Down. Their servants were often accompanied by a youth called McClory, who drove his own cart. McClory and Brontë, who were about the same age, resembled each other in the fiery colour of their hair. They became fast friends, and it was arranged that Brontë should visit McClory in County Down during the Christmas holidays.

CHAPTER X

LOVE AT FIRST SIGHT

THE visit to McClory's house in County Down was another momentous step in the life of Hugh Brontë. He had shaken off the nightmare of cruel slavery. His work, mostly in the open air, suited him. He was well paid, had good food and clothing, and in two years the starved and ragged boy had become a large, handsome, well-dressed man. Like most handsome people, Hugh knew that he was handsome, and the resources of Dundalk were taxed in those days to the utmost to set off to perfection his manly and stately figure.

On Christmas Eve Hugh Brontë drove up furiously in a Newry gig to the house of McClory in Ballynaskeagh. He was becoming a somewhat vain man, and fond of admiration ; and no doubt, as he approached McClory's thatched cottage, with his pockets full of money, and with the self-confidence which prosperity breeds, he meant to flutter the house with his magnificence.

But a surprise was in store for him. The cottage

door was opened in response to his somewhat boisterous knock by a young woman of dazzling beauty. Hugh Brontë, previous to his flight, had seen few women except his aunt Mary, and in the days of his freedom he had become acquainted only with lodging-house keepers, and County Louth women, who carried their fowls and eggs to Dundalk fairs and markets. He had scarcely ever seen a comely girl, and never in his life any one who had any attractions for him.

The simply dressed, artless girl who opened the door was probably the prettiest girl in County Down at the time. On this point there is absolute unanimity in all the statements that have reached me. The words " Irish beauty and pure Celt " have often been used in describing her.

Her hair, which hung in a profusion of ringlets round her shoulders, was luminous gold. Her forehead was Parian marble. Her evenly set teeth were lustrous pearls, and the roses of health glowed on her cheeks. She had the long dark-brown eyelashes that in Ireland so often accompany golden hair, and her deep hazel eyes had the violet tint and melting expression which in a diluted form descended to her granddaughters, and made the plain and irregular features of the Brontë girls really attractive. The eyes also contained the lambent fire that Mrs. Gaskell noticed in Charlotte's eyes, ready to flash indignation and

LOVE AT FIRST SIGHT 81

scorn. She had a tall and stately figure, with head well poised above a graceful neck and well-formed bust ; but she did not communicate these graces of form to her granddaughters. There are people still living who remember the stately old woman " Ayles " Brontë, as she was called by her neighbours in her old age.

Hugh Brontë was completely unmanned by the radiant beauty of the simple country girl who appeared before him. He stood awkwardly staring at her with his mouth open, fumbling with his hat, and trying in vain to say something. At last he stammered out a question about Mr. McClory, and the girl, who was Alice McClory, told him that her brother would soon be home, and invited him into the house.

He entered blushing and feeling uncomfortable, but the unaffected simplicity of Alice McClory's manner soon put him at his ease, and before the brother Patrick, known afterwards as " Red Paddy," had returned home Hugh was madly and hopelessly in love with his sister.

Like his son the Rev. Patrick Brontë in England, and like the Irish curate who proposed marriage to Charlotte on the strength of one night's acquaintance, Hugh, dazzled by beauty and blinded by love, declared his passion before he had discovered any signs of mutual liking, or had any evidence that his advances would be agreeable.

Alice, in a simple but cold and business-like manner, told him that she did not yet know him, but that, as he was a Protestant and she a Catholic, there was an insuperable bar between them. Hugh urged that he himself had no religion, never having darkened a church door, and that he was quite willing to be anything she wished him to be.

Alice met his earnest pleadings with playful sallies, which disconcerted him, and little by little she led him to the story of his life, episodes of which she had heard from her brother. Sympathy leads to love, and Alice was moved greatly by Hugh's simple narrative.

CHAPTER XI

TRUE LOVE AND PARTY STRIFE

THE Christmas holidays passed pleasantly under the hospitable roof of the McClory family. The chief amusement of the neighbourhood was drinking in a *shebeen*, or local public-house ; but Hugh declined to accompany Paddy to the *shebeen*, preferring to share his sister's solitude.

Before the holidays had come to a close Hugh and Alice had become engaged, but the course of true love in their case was destined to the proverbial fate. All Miss McClory's friends were scandalised at the thought of her consenting to marry a Protestant.

Religion among Catholics and Orangemen in those days consisted largely of party hatred. He was a good Protestant who, sober as well as drunk, cursed the Pope on the 12th of July, wore orange colours, and played with fife and drum a tune known as the *Battle of the Boyne* ; and he was a good Catholic who, in whatever condition, used equally emphatic language regarding King William.

No more genuine expression of religious feeling was looked for on either side.

There is a story told in the McClory district which illustrates the current religious sentiment. Two brother Orangemen, good men after their lights, had long been fast friends. They seldom missed an opportunity, in the presence of Catholics, of consigning the Pope to the uncomfortable place to which he himself has been wont to consign heretics.

It happened that one of the two Orangemen fell sick, and when he was at the point of death his friend became greatly concerned about his spiritual state and visited him. He found him in an unconscious condition and sinking fast, and, putting his lips close to the ear of his sick friend, he asked him to give him a sign that he felt spiritually happy. The dying man, with a last supreme effort, raised his voice above a whisper, and in the venerable and well-known formula cursed the Pope. His friend was comforted, believing that all was well.

Whether this gruesome story be true or not, it goes to illustrate the fact that blasphemous bigotry had largely usurped the place of religion. But bitter party feeling did not end with mere words. Bloody battles between Orangemen and Catholics were periodically fought on the 12th of July, the anniversary of the battle of the Boyne,

TRUE LOVE AND PARTY STRIFE 85

and on the 17th of March, St. Patrick's Day. Within six miles of McClory's house more than a dozen pitched battles were fought, sometimes with scythes tied on poles, and sometimes with firearms. One of these murderous onsets, known as the battle of Ballynafern, took place within sight of McClory's house.

At Dolly's Brae a battle was fought in 1849 in presence of a large body of troops and constabulary, who remained neutral spectators of the conflict till the Catholics fled, and then the constabulary joined with the victors in firing on the flying foe.

The scenes of these struggles, such as Tillyorier, Katesbridge, Hilltown, the Diamond, etc., are classic spots now. Each has had its poet, and ballads are sung to celebrate the prowess of the victors, who were uniformly the Orangemen, inasmuch as they used firearms, while the Catholics generally fought with pikes and scythes.

Hugh Brontë had not yet discovered the deep and wide gulf that yawned between Protestants and Catholics, and so he made light of the religious objections of which he had heard so much from Alice.

But the Catholic friends of Miss McClory, who had heard the Pope cursed by Protestant lips almost every day of their lives, could not stand by and see a Catholic lamb removed into the Protestant shambles. They came to look on Brontë as a Protestant emissary, more influenced by a fiendish desire to plunder the Catholic fold than by love for their beautiful relative.

Hugh Brontë in his eager simplicity wanted to supersede all opposition by getting married immediately, but so great a commotion ensued that he had to return to the kilns at Mount Pleasant, leaving his matrimonial prospects in a very unsatisfactory condition.

Troops of relatives invaded the McClory house daily, and ardent Catholics tried in vain to argue down Alice McClory's newly kindled love. All the Roman Catholic neighbours joined in giving copious advice, and little was talked of at fairs and markets and chapel but the proposed marriage of Alice McClory to an unknown Protestant heretic.

The priest also, as family friend, was drawn into the matter. In those days Irish priests were educated in France or Italy, and were generally men of culture and refinement. Their horizon had been widened. They had come in contact with the language, literature, and social habits of other peoples, and they had become courteous men of the world. They had to some extent got out of touch with the fierce fanaticism of Irish party strife.

The priest called on Miss McClory. Everybody

TRUE LOVE AND PARTY STRIFE 87

knew that he had, and awaited the result; but Alice's beauty and simplicity and tears made such an impression on the kind-hearted old priest, that his chivalrous instinct was aroused, and he was almost won to the lady's side. The centre of the agitation then shifted from McClory's cottage to the priest's manse, and so hot was the anger of the infuriated Catholics that the good-natured priest promised, sorely against his will, that he would not consent to marry the pair.

Hugh Brontë was nominally a Protestant, but he had not been in a church of any kind from the time he was five or six years of age; he had received no religious instruction; he could not read the Bible for himself, and no one had ever read it to him; and he was as innocent of any religious bias or bigotry as a savage in Central Africa. Suddenly he found himself the chief figure in a fierce religious drama.

At first he was greatly amused, and laughed at the very suggestion of his religion being considered a stumbling-block. From the time he left his father's house he had seldom heard the Divine name pronounced except in some form of malediction, and religion had brought no consolation to his hard life.

He had never presumed to think that he had any relationship to the Church, its priests were so gorgeous and its people so well-to-do. Gallagher

88 *THE BRONTËS IN IRELAND*

had made him familiar with the dread powers of the infernal world, and with "the Blessed Virgin and the saints" in their malevolent capacity; but the malignant hypocrisy of Gallagher was quite as repulsive to him as the vindictive blasphemy of his uncle. In fact, he had lived in an atmosphere untouched by the light or warmth of religion.

Hugh's bondage and suffering had made him neither cringing nor cruel, and his freedom had come in time to permit the full development of a large and generous heart in a robust and healthy body. In his simplicity of heart he prevailed on Alice to invite her friends to meet him. He would soon remove their dislike with regard to his religion. Under the impulse of his enthusiasm he thought he could disarm prejudice by a frank and open avowal of his absolute indifference to all religions.

Nothing perhaps in the whole history of the Brontës exceeded in interest that meeting. A dozen wily Ulster Catholics gathered round simple-hearted Hugh Brontë in Paddy McClory's kitchen. How the Orange champions would have trembled for the Protestant cause if they had been aware of Hugh's danger!

The preliminary salutations over, a black bottle was produced and a glass of whiskey handed round. Hugh had never learned to drink whiskey, and at that time detested the very smell of it.

TRUE LOVE AND PARTY STRIFE 89

His refusal to drink with McClory's friends was the first ground of offence, but the whiskey had not yet brought the drinkers into the quarrelsome mood.

When several bottles of McClory's whiskey had been drunk, and the temperature of the guests had risen proportionately, the religious question was approached. Brontë was urged in peremptory tones to abjure Protestantism. He had his answer ready. He was no more a Protestant than they were, and he had no Protestantism to abjure. 'Will you then curse King William?" said a fiery little man who had taken much liquor, and seemed to be the spokesman of the party.

There is a principle in human nature which has been taken far too little account of by both philosophers and peasants. It has been the dominant principle in many of the important decisions that have sealed the fate of nations as well as of individuals. The principle is expressed by a word which is always pronounced in one way by the cultured, and in quite a different way by the unlettered. The word in its illiterate use is " con*trairy*ness," and but for the principle expressed by this word the Brontë girls would never have made their mark in literature, and this history would never have been written.

" Curse King William !" shouted the fiery little man, supported by a hoarse echo from the other half-tipsy guests, all of whom had turned fierce and glowing eyes on the supposed Protestant.

" I cannot curse King William," replied Hugh, smiling. " He never did me any harm ; besides, he is beyond the region of my blessings and cursings ; but," he added, warming with his subject, " I should not mind cursing the Pope, if he is the author of your fierce and besotted religion."

Alice first saw the danger, and uttered a sharp cry. Suddenly the family party sprang upon Hugh as the ambushed Philistines once flung themselves on Samson ; but he shook them off, and left them sprawling on the floor. Alice drew him from the house, bleeding and dishevelled, and after a tender parting in the grove beside the stream he started on foot for Mount Pleasant.

Two immediate results followed that conflict: Hugh Brontë became a furious Protestant and a frantic lover. There was no lukewarmness or indifference as to his Protestantism. The Brontë *contrairyness* had met the kind of opposition to give it a stubborn set, and he there and then became a Protestant double-dyed in the warp and in the woof.

The process of his conversion, such as it was, was prompt, decisive, effectual. It was in its early stages Orange in hue and militant in fibre, and was a genuine product of the times.

Hugh's love for Alice was fanned into a fierce

TRUE LOVE AND PARTY STRIFE 91

flame by the events of that night. When he first met her he had been dazzled by her rare beauty. He had seen few women, and never one like Alice, For the first time he had come under the spell of a simple and beautiful girl. They were young, shy lovers; very happy in each other's company, but each sufficiently self-possessed to be happy enough in self.

From the furnace of contradiction on that night the jewel love had leaped forth. Each was drawn out from the self-centre in which each had been concentrated in self; he to declare his love in the face of relentless foes, and she to cling to him and protect him when bruised and torn by her friends.

Beneath the pines that night they pledged with mingling tears undying love. They parted, but their hearts were one; and persecution, poverty, and bereavement only welded them more closely together in the changing years.*

* For much that is vivid in this scene I am indebted to a younger Paddy McClory. He was an old, and most intelligent servant of Mr. McKee's, and died some years ago at a very great age. He was a Roman Catholic, and had a son killed in the battle of Ballynafern.

CHAPTER XII

LOVE'S SUBTERFUGES

HUGH returned to the Mount Pleasant Kilns, but his heart was no longer in his work. The burning of lime requires incessant care. The limestones must be broken to a proper size, layers of coal in due proportion must be added, and there must be constant watchfulness lest the fires should die out. Farmers' sons and servants started generally from County Down about midnight, and after travelling all night arrived at the kilns for their loads about dawn. A badly burnt kiln of lime was a grave loss to the owners, as well as a serious disappointment to the customers, and likely to result in loss of custom.

There were many complaints as to the character of the lime immediately after Christmas, and the farmers on several occasions found on *slaking* their loads at home that only the surface of the stones was burnt, and that they had paid for and imported heaps of raw limestone.

Hugh's thoughts were not in his business. He had made several Sunday journeys to Ballynaskeagh to have secret meetings with Alice. They met in the grove by the brook, in a spot still

THE COURTING BOWER.

pointed out as the "Lover's Arbour" or "Courting Bower," and there, under willows festooned with ivy and honeysuckle and sweetbriar, they spent lonely but happy Sundays.

They were at last betrayed by a Catholic servant,

who had been entrusted with a letter to Alice. Then began a system of espionage and petty persecution, and all the forces of the McClory clan were united in an effort to compel Alice to marry a Catholic neighbour called Joe Burns.

At this time Hugh began to learn to read and write, and he succeeded so far by the light from the eye of the kiln at night as to be able to write love-letters which Alice was able to read. He also about the same time succeeded in spelling his way through the New Testament.

News from the north had reached his fellow-workers that he was a Protestant firebrand, that he had cursed the Pope, and made a savage attack on some harmless Catholics. At the kilns his manner had changed, and he had become moody and morose. Besides, he was constantly reading a little book by the light of the burning lime at night, instead of telling stories and singing songs, as in former times. The book was said to be the Bible; but it was, in fact, the New Testament.

A plot was immediately hatched to get rid of so dangerous a colleague. One of the Catholics undertook, as usual, to look after the kilns while Hugh made an expedition to County Down; but he not only failed to charge the kilns properly, but sent for the owner on Monday morning early that he might see for himself the condition of things.

The northern carts arrived by dawn, to find

LOVE'S SUBTERFUGES

that there was nothing for them but unburnt lime. While the matter was being explained Hugh arrived, haggard and weary after his night's journey, and was peremptorily dismissed, without any explanation from either side being tendered or accepted.

I have no record of Hugh's proceedings immediately after his dismissal, but he must have been reduced to considerable straits, for he went to the hiring ground in Newry, and engaged himself as a common servant-boy to a farmer who resided in Donoughmore. As a farm labourer in those days he would receive about £6 per annum, with board and lodging ; but, then, he was near his Alice, and that made every burden light.

Hugh's new master, James Harshaw, was not an ordinary farmer. The Harshaws had occupied the farm from early in the fifteenth century, and James, who had received the education of a gentleman, had behind him the traditions of an old and respectable family. In the Harshaws' home shrewd and steady industry was brightened by culture and refinement. The wheel of fortune had brought Hugh Brontë into a family where mental alacrity had full play.

Brontë seems to have been treated with consideration and kindness by the Harshaws, who probably recognised in him something superior to the ordinary farm-servant. At any rate, in those days the walls of class distinction were not raised so high as now, and the Harshaw children taught him to read.

Hugh was much with the family. He drove them to Donoughmore Presbyterian Meeting House on Sundays, and sat with them in their pew, and he accompanied them to rustic singing parties and such local gatherings. He used to drive them in the summer-time to Warrenpoint and Newcastle, and other watering-places, and remain with them as their attendant.

In such treatment of a servant there was nothing unusual, and Mr. John Harshaw, the present proprietor of the ancestral home, has no very decisive information regarding this particular servant. He says : " The probability is that Hugh Brontë hired with my grandfather, whose land touched the Lough ; but I fear it is too true that he passed through my grandfather's service and left no permanent record behind him."

I think it is more than probable that Brontë repaid his young masters and mistresses for their teaching by telling them stories. Under Harshaw's roof he found not only work and shelter, but a home and comfort ; and it is inconceivable that under those circumstances he allowed the gift that was in him of charming by vivid narration to lie dormant.

As long as he lived he spoke of the Harshaws

LOVE'S SUBTERFUGES 97

with gratitude and affection, and I do not believe
he could have been so glad and happy without
contributing to the general enjoyment.

In the latter part of the last century the *raconteur*
occupied the place in Ireland now taken by the
modern novel, and I believe Hugh Brontë dropped
doctrine into the minds of the young Harshaws
which produced far-reaching results. Such was
the fixed conviction of my old teacher, the Rev.
William McAllister.

It happened that the Martins, another ancient
family, lived quite near to the Harshaws. The
land of the two families enclosed Loughorne Lough
round. The Martins were rich and somewhat aristocratic; but the two families were thrown much
together, and Samuel Martin, the son of the one
house, married Jane Harshaw, the daughter of the
other.

She was a deeply religious and resolute woman,
with a stern sense of duty. One of her nephews,
the Rev. R. H. Harshaw, tells me she always
conducted family worship after the death of her
husband. She died of a fever, caught while
ministering to the dying, in accordance with her
high sense of Christian duty. Her life was given
for others, and at her funeral the Rev. S. J.
Moore summed up her character as "a woman
who knew her duty, and did it."

Her second son, John Martin, inherited his

mother's great mental capacity and strong sense of duty. At school in Newry he met young John Mitchell, and inspired him with something of his own enthusiasm, and the two youths came to the conclusion that it was their duty to put right Ireland's wrongs. John Mitchell was sent to penal servitude for fifteen or twenty years, and then John Martin stepped into the place vacated by his friend, and was transported to Van Diemen's Land for ten years.

The conviction of "honest John Martin" gave a blow to the old system in Ireland from which it has never recovered. Even his enemies were shocked at the severity of the sentence ; but, then, he had written a pamphlet under the text, " *Your land, strangers devour it in your presence, and it is desolate*" (Isa. i. 7). He had proclaimed from the housetops Hugh Brontë's tenant-right doctrines, of which more anon. He had attacked the sacred rights of landlordism, and he was sent to a safe and distant place for quite a different offence, called " treason felony."

John Martin was a man of large property, but he devoted his life and all his income to what he considered the good of others. He had taken his B.A. degree at Trinity College, Dublin, and studied medicine, and for many years he gave advice and drugs gratuitously to all who came to him. The poor were passionately attached to him.

LOVE'S SUBTERFUGES

I remember seeing him and speaking to him after he had received a free pardon and become a member of Parliament. No one could have looked on the fine capacious head, and the handsome benevolent face, without questioning the system that had no better use for such a man than sending him to rot in penal servitude.

Lord Palmerston beheld the ex-convict with profound admiration, and expressed deep sympathy with him as the victim of a bad system.

John Martin preached and suffered for the very doctrines that Hugh Brontë enunciated with such passionate conviction. Where did he get those doctrines? I think there is no doubt that John Martin's beliefs and principles grew from seeds sown by Hugh Brontë, the servant-boy, in the sympathetic mind of his mother.

Jane Harshaw, however she got them, carried the doctrines into the Martin family. They mingled with and strengthened her strong sense of duty, and they added passion to her zeal for justice and the thing that was right.

With her son John the feeling of obligation to break the ban of Ireland's curse became irresistible. He was dowered with an inexhaustible grace of pity for all sufferers, and the impulse to redress the wrongs of the oppressed overpowered him, and led him to acts of impatience and imprudence which gave his cool-headed enemies the opportunity they

THE BRONTËS IN IRELAND

were ready enough to embrace. But the revolutionary doctrines for which John Martin suffered came from the same seed that produced Charlotte Brontë's radical sentiments, and it is interesting to note that in both cases the seed produced its fruit about the same period (1847—1848).

I must now leave these historical speculations, however plausible and probable they. may be, and return to the direct narration of known facts.

Hugh Brontë had disappeared for ever from the Mount Pleasant Kilns. Those who had plotted his dismissal exaggerated every foible of his life, and invented others after he was gone, until by a spiteful blending of fact and fancy they made him into a monster.

The farmers' sons and servants who carted lime from Mount Pleasant to County Down brought with them wonderful tales of his misdeeds and disgrace, and Alice McClory's guardians believed that he had disappeared for ever into the distant south whence he had emerged. They never suspected that he was actually living in their neighbourhood, and that he and Alice had met at Warrenpoint, Newcastle, and elsewhere.

Under restraint Alice had drooped and pined, but now that Brontë had left the country she was permitted to ride about the neighbourhood quite alone. She enjoyed horse exercise greatly, but no matter in what direction she left home her way lay

LOVE'S SUBTERFUGES 101

always through Loughorne. Perhaps the roads were better in that direction, but she always exchanged salutations with a handsome working man by the expanse of water in Loughorne.

When he was not about she was wont very humanely to take her horse down to the lake to drink, and from a hole in an old tree she used to remove a scrap of paper, leaving something instead. The tree used to be pointed out as " Brontë's postbox "; but the lake has recently been drained, and the tree has, I believe, disappeared.

Everything that could be done was done to please Miss McClory, but no opportunity was missed to further Farmer Burns's suit. He was a prosperous man. He had a good farm, a good house, plenty of horses and cows and pigs, and was a very desirable husband for Alice. He was also a Catholic. Brontë had shown that he did not care for her by going away and never thinking of her more. The priest joined with Alice's female friends in pleading for Burns. At length by dogged perseverance they prevailed on her to consent to marry Burns and forget Brontë. The incessant drip had made an impression at last, and the crafty relatives had gained their end.

There was joy in the Catholic camp when it was publicly announced that Miss McClory and Mr. Burns were soon to be married. McClory's house was thatched anew, and whitewashed and renovated throughout, the roses were nailed up round the windows, the street was strewn with fresh sand, new window-blinds and bed-curtains were provided, and pots and pans were burnished.

Never before had McClory's house been subjected to such an outburst of sweeping and brushing and washing and scouring; the whole place became redolent of potash and suds. It was spring-cleaning *in excelsis.*

The local dressmaker, Annie McCabe, whose great-granddaughter of the same name is now dressmaker of the same place, assisted by Miss McClory's female relatives, was busily engaged on the bridal dress. Burns used to look in daily on the incessant preparations, his countenance beaming with joy; but Alice would not permit him to destroy the pleasures of imagination by approaching near to her. She would lift her finger coyly, and warn him off if he presumed on any familiarities; but she allowed him to sit on the other side of the kitchen fire from that graced by herself.

At length the wedding day arrived. Such signs of feasting had never before been seen in Ballynaskeagh. New loaves had been procured from Newry, fresh beef from Rathfriland, whiskey from Banbridge; a great pudding, composed of flour and potatoes, and boiled for many hours over a slow fire with hot coals on the lid of the oven, had been prepared; two of the largest turkeys

LOVE'S SUBTERFUGES

had been boiled, and laid out on great dishes, with an abundant coating of melted butter ; and a huge roll of roast beef was served up as a burnt-offering. Signs of abundance stood on table and dresser and hob, while rows of bottles peeped from behind the window curtains, and neither envy nor spite could say that Paddy McClory was not providing a splendid wedding for his sister.

The morning rose glorious, and as the custom then was, Burns and his friends, mounted on their best horses, raced to the house of the bride *for the broth*, first in being the winner. On such occasions crowds of neighbours crowned the hill-tops. The cavalcade was greeted with ringing cheers as it swept in a cloud of dust down the road from the Knock Hill. Several riders were unhorsed, but the steeds arrived in McClory's court champing their bits and covered with foam.

A covered car from Newry stood near the house on the road to take Alice to the chapel ; but she was to ride away from the chapel mounted on the pillion behind her husband.

There was an unexpected pause, no one knew why. Some dismounted, and stood by their stirrups, ready to mount when the bride had entered her carriage. Glasses of whiskey were handed round, and then the pause became more awkward and the suspense more intense.

At last it became known that Alice, who had been

up nearly all night finishing her new gowns, had felt weary, and, fitting on her wedding dress, had gone out on her mare for a spurt to shake off drowsiness. Messengers were sent in different directions to search for her, but they had not returned. Some accident must have befallen her.

Burns, who rode a powerful black horse and who had won the broth, galloped off wildly towards Loughbrickland. The other cavaliers scoured the country in different directions; but while all kinds of surmises were being hazarded, a messenger on foot from Banbridge with dainties for the feast arrived, and reported that he had met Miss McClory and a tall gentleman galloping furiously towards the river Bann near Banbridge.

There was great excitement among the wedding party, and whiskey and strong language without measure. After a hurried consultation the mounted guests agreed to pursue the fugitives and bring Miss McClory back; but while they were tightening their girths and getting ready for a gallop of five or six miles, a boy rode up to the house on the mare that had been ridden by Alice, bearing a letter to say she had just been married to Hugh Brontë in Magherally Church. She sent her love and grateful thanks to her brother, hoped the party would enjoy the wedding dinner, and begged them to drink her health as Mrs. Brontë.

The plucky manner in which the lady had

LOVE'S SUBTERFUGES

carried out her own plan, outwitting the coercionists by her own cleverness, called forth admiration in the midst of disappointment, and the cheery message touched every heart. The calamity that had befallen Burns did not weigh heavily on the hearts of the guests in presence of the splendid dinner before them, and especially as it was now clear that the lady was being forced to marry him against her will.

At this juncture the kind and courteous old priest rose, and with great skill and good humour talked about the events of the day. He brought into special prominence the humorous and heroic episode in a manner that appealed to the chivalry of his hearers, and then with tender pathos, referring to the beautiful daughter of the house, called upon the guests to drink her health. The toast was responded to with a hearty, ringing cheer.

Burns, who has left a good reputation behind him, promptly proposed prosperity to the new married couple ; and Red Paddy, always kind and generous, promised to send the united good wishes of the whole party to the bride and bridegroom, and to assure them of a hearty welcome in which the past would be forgotten. Paddy, as we shall see, kept his word. Thus the grandfather and grandmother of the great novelists were married in 1776 in the Protestant Church of Magherally, the clergyman who officiated pronouncing the bride the most beautiful woman he had ever seen.

CHAPTER XIII

LOVE IN A COTTAGE

AFTER a brief honeymoon spent at Warren-point, Alice Brontë returned, on her brother's invitation, to her old home, and Hugh went back to complete his term of service in Loughorne. It soon became desirable that his wife should have a home of her own, and he took a cottage in Emdale in the parish of Drumballyroney, with which Drumgooland was united at the time.

The house stands near cross-roads leading to important towns. In a direct line it is about three and three-quarters statute miles from Rathfriland, seven and three-quarters from Newry, twelve from Warrenpoint, and five and a quarter from Banbridge. The map shows the position of the house on the north-west side of the old road, leading in Hugh Brontë's day to Newry and Warrenpoint. Almost opposite on the other side of the road there was a blacksmith's shop, which still continues to be a blacksmith's shop. The Brontë house remains, though partially in ruins. I have given a photo-

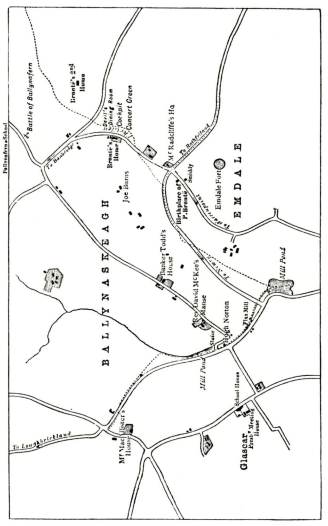

THE BRONTË DISTRICT.

LOVE IN A COTTAGE 109

graph of it taken from the Banbridge side. It stands as frontispiece.

The house is now used as a byre, but its dimensions are exactly the same as when it became the home of Hugh Brontë and his bride. The rent then would be about sixpence per week, and would in accordance with the general custom be paid by one day's work in the week, the work being given in the busy seasons.

The house consisted of two rooms. That over which the roof still stands was without chimney, and was used as bedroom and parlour; and the outer room, from which the roof has fallen, was used as a corn-kiln and also as kitchen and reception-room.

A farmer's wife, whose ancestors lived close to the Brontë house long before the Brontës were heard of in County Down, pointing to a spot in the corner of the byre opposite to the window, said, " There is the very spot where the Rev. Patrick Brontë was born." Then she added, " Numbers of great folk have asked me about his birthplace, but, och! how could I tell them that any dacent man was ever born in such a place!" This feeling on the part of the neighbours will probably account for the fact that everything written thus far regarding Patrick Brontë's birthplace is wrong, neither the townland nor even the parish of his birth being correctly given.

In the lowly cottage in Emdale, now known as "The Kiln," and used as a cowshed, Patrick Brontë was born on the 17th of March, 1777. Men have risen to fame from a lowly origin ; but few men have ever emerged from humbler circumstances than Patrick Brontë.

Many a reader of Mrs. Gaskell's life of Charlotte Brontë has been saddened by the picture of the vicar's daughters amid their narrow and grim surroundings ; but the grey vicarage of Haworth was a palace compared with the hovel in which the vicar himself was born and reared.

Besides, the Haworth vicarage was never really as sombre as Mrs. Gaskell painted it, for Miss Ellen Nussey was a constant visitor, and she assures me that the girls were bright and happy in their home, always engaged on some project of absorbing interest, and always enjoying life in their own sober and thoughtful way.

The Brontë cottage in Emdale was very poor, but it was brightened with the perennial sunshine of love. It was love in a cottage, in which the bare walls and narrow board were golden in the light of Alice Brontë's smile. It was said in the neighbourhood that Mrs. Brontë's smile "would have tamed a mad bull." And on her deathbed she thanked God that her husband had never looked upon her with a frown.

In their wedded love they were very poor, but

LOVE IN A COTTAGE 111

very happy. Hugh's constant, steady work provided for the daily wants of an ever-increasing family, but it made no provision for the strain of adverse circumstances. In fact, the Emdale Brontës lived like birds, and as happy as birds.

Hugh Brontë was one of the industrious poor. The salt of his life was honest, manly toil. He had forgotten the luxury of his childhood's home, and he did not feel any degradation in his lowly lot.

In our artificial civilisation we have come to place too much store on the accident of wealth. Our blessed Saviour, whom the rich and luxurious as well as the poor call " Lord," was born in as lowly a condition of comfortless poverty as Patrick Brontë. Cows are now housed in Brontë's birthplace, but our Lord was born among the animals in the caravanserai. And yet in our social code we have reduced the Decalogue to the one commandment, " Thou shalt not be poor."

Hugh Brontë did not choose poverty as his lot, but being a working man, like the Carpenter of Nazareth, he did the daily work that came to his hand, and then side by side with Alice he found the fulness of each day sufficient for all its wants.

The happy home was soon crowded with children, and the family removed to a larger and better house in the townland of Lisnacreevy.

The following verses have always been known

THE BRONTËS IN IRELAND

as the product of Hugh Brontë's muse. I am inclined to think they may have, in an original form, been produced by Hugh, and smoothed down by his son Patrick ; and perhaps in the refining process they have lost in strength more than they have gained in sound.

I do not think old Hugh would have known anything at first hand of the "peach-bloom," or of "blood-red Mars." The poem forty years ago had many variations, but there is one line of special interest, as it shows that the verses were known to Charlotte Brontë. The verse with a slight variation is put into the mouth of Jane Eyre. Rochester says, "Jane suits me : do I suit her?" Jane answers, "To the finest fibre of my nature, sir."

"ALICE AND HUGH.

" The red rose paled before the blush
    That mantled o'er thy dimpled cheek ;
The peach-bloom faded at the flush
    That tinged thy beauty ripe and meek.

" Thy milk-white brow outshone the snow,
    Thy lustrous eyes outglanced the stars ;
Thy cherry lips, with love aglow,
    Burned ruddier than the blood-red Mars.

" Thy sweet, low voice waked in my heart
    Dead memories of my mother's love ;
My long-lost sister's artless art
    Lived in thy smiles, my gentle dove.

LOVE IN A COTTAGE

"Dear Alice, how thy charm and grace
    Kindled my dull and stagnant life!
From first I saw thy winning face
    My whole heart claimed thee for my wife.

"I thought you'd make me happy, dear,
    I sought you for my very own ;
You clung to me through storm and fear,
    You loved me still, though poor and lone.

"My love was centred all in self,
    Thy love was centred all in me ;
True wife above all pride and pelf,
    My life's deep current flows for thee.

"The finest fibres of my soul
    Entwine with thine in love's strong fold,
Our tin cup is a golden bowl,
    Love fills our cot with wealth untold."

CHAPTER XIV

THE DAILY ROUND

HUGH BRONTË and his wife could not live wholly on love in a cottage, and Hugh had to bestir himself. He was an unskilled labourer, though he understood the art of burning lime. There was no limestone, however, in that part of County Down to burn, and as he could not have a lime-kiln he resolved to have a corn-kiln.

At the beginning of this century a corn-kiln in such a district in Ireland was a very simple affair. A floor of earthenware tiles, pierced nearly through from the under side, was arranged as a kind of platform or loft. Beneath there was a furnace, which was heated by burning the rough, dry seeds, or outer *shelling*, which had been ground off the oats. In front of the furnace there was a hollow, called the " logie-hole," in which the kiln-man sat, with the *shelling*, or seeds, heaped up within arm's length around him, and with his right hand he *beeked* the kiln by throwing, every few seconds, a sprinkling of seeds on the flame. In this

THE DAILY ROUND

way he kept up a warm glow under the corn till it was sufficiently dry for the mill.

Such was the simple character of the ordinary corn-kiln in County Down at the beginning of the century. But I have been assured, by old men of the neighbourhood, that Hugh Brontë's kiln was of a still more primitive structure. The platform, or corn-floor, was constructed by laying down iron bars across unhewn stones set up on end. On these bars straw matting was placed, and on the matting the corn was spread to dry. Such a structure was the immediate precursor of the pottery-floored kiln. The design was the same in both, but the matting was always liable to catch fire, and required careful attention.

The kiln was erected in the part of the Brontë cottage now roofless, and, like the cottage itself, must have been a very humble erection. It has been suggested that the kiln may have stood elsewhere ; but it is now established beyond all doubt, by the investigations of the Rev. W. J. McCracken, and the unanimous testimony of the inhabitants, that the Brontë kiln stood in the ruined room of the Brontë cottage, and, in fact, it is known by the name of " Brontë's kiln."

Within those walls, now roofless, the grandfather of Charlotte Brontë began, in 1776, to earn the daily bread of himself and his bride by roasting his neighbours' oats. His wage was known by

THE BRONTËS IN IRELAND

the name of *muther*, and consisted of so many pounds of fresh oats taken from every hundred-weight brought to him to be kiln-dried. The miller, too, was paid in kind; but his *muther* was taken by measure after the *shellings*, or seeds, had been ground off the grain.

When Hugh Brontë had accumulated a sackful of *muther*, he dried it on his kiln, took it to the mill, and paid his *muther* in turn to the miller to have it ground into meal. The meal, when taken home, was stored in a barrel, and with the produce of the rood of potatoes which Hugh had *sod* on his brother-in-law's farm, became the food of himself and family.

As the Brontës could not consume all the *muther* themselves, the surplus would be sold to provide clothing and other necessaries; and though there remains no trace of pigsty or fowl-house around the cottage, there can be little doubt that Mrs. Brontë would have both pigs and fowl to eke out her husband's earnings.

Mrs. Brontë was a famous spinner, and she handed down the art to her daughters. She had always a couple of sheep grazing on her brother's land. She carded and span the wool, her spinning-wheel singing all day beside her husband as he *beeked* the kiln. Then, during the long dark evenings, when they had no light but the red eye of the kiln, she knitted the yarn into hose and vests and

THE DAILY ROUND

shirts, and even headgear, so that Hugh Brontë, like his sons in after-years, was almost wholly clad in " home-spun."

This probably had something to do with the general impression, which still remains in the neighbourhood, of the stately and shapely forms of the Brontë men and women. The knitted woollen garments fitted close, unlike the fantastic and shapeless habiliments that came from the hands of the local tailors in those days.

Alice Brontë also span nearly all the garments which she wore, and her tall and comely daughters after her were dressed in clothes which their own hands had taken from the fleece.

From choice as well as from necessity the Brontës wore woollen garments, and the vicar carried the same taste with him to England, where his dislike of everything made of cotton was attributed by his biographer to dread of fire.

The absurd servant's gossip as to his cutting up and destroying his wife's silk gown had possibly a grain of truth in it, owing to his preference for woollen garments ; but the atrocity manufactured out of the gossip by Mrs. Gaskell was probably an exaggeration of an innocent act. At any rate, the old vicar characterised the statement, I believe truly, by a small but ugly word.

All the Brontës, father, mother, sons, and daughters, to the number of twelve, were clad in wool, and they were said to be the "healthiest, handsomest, strongest, heartiest family in the whole country." They were a standing proof of the excellency of the woollen theory; and it is interesting to note how Hugh Brontë's theory and practice have received approval in our own day.

For a time the Brontës had to look to others to weave their yarn into the blankets and friezes that they required; but Patrick was taught to weave, and then his father's household manufactured for themselves out of the raw staple everything they wore, from the drugget petticoat to the fine and gracefully-fitting corset.

Even the scarlet mantle, for which "Ayles" Brontë is still remembered in Ballynaskeagh, was carded, spun, knitted, and dyed by Mrs. Brontë's own hands. The spirit of independence manifested by the Brontës in England was a survival of a still sturdier spirit that had its origin in one of the humblest cabins in County Down.

As time passed Hugh Brontë became a famous ditcher. There is a very old man called Hugh Norton living in Ballynaskeagh who remembers him making fences and philosophising at the same time. It is very probable that the introduction of corn-kilns constructed of burnt pottery may have left him without custom for his straw-mat kiln, just as the introduction of machinery at a later period left the country hand-looms idle.

In Hugh Brontë's time more careful attention began to be given to the land. Bogs were drained, fields were fenced, roads constructed, bridges made, houses built, with greater energy than had ever been known before ; and although the landlord generally raised the rent on every improvement effected by the tenant, the wave of prosperity and improvement continued.

Hugh Brontë was a good steady workman, and found constant employment, and at that time wages rose from sixpence per day to eightpence and tenpence.

The *sod* fences made by him still stand as a monument of honest work, and there are few country districts where huntsmen would find greater difficulty with the fences than in Emdale and Ballynaskeagh.

As Hugh Brontë advanced in life he continued to prosper. He removed, as we have said, from the Emdale cottage to a larger house in Lisna-creevy, and from there he and his family went home to live with Red Paddy, Mrs. Brontë's brother. On the Ballynaskeagh farm the children found full scope for their energies, and they continued to prosper until they were in very comfortable circumstances.

The Brontës were greatly advanced in their prosperity by a discovery made by John Loudon MacAdam. He wrote several treatises on road-making of a revolutionary character. His proposal was to make roads by laying down layers of broken stones, which he said would become hardened into a solid mass by the traffic passing over them.

For a time he was the subject of much ridicule, but he persevered, and proved his theory in a practical fashion. The importance of the invention was subsequently acknowledged by a grant from the Government of £10,000, which he accepted, and by the offer of a baronetcy, which he declined. He lived to see the world's highways improved by his discovery, and the English language enriched by his name.

The old, unscientific road-makers were too conservative to engage in the construction of macadamised roads; but the Brontës were shrewd enough to see the value of the new method, and they tendered for county contracts, and their tenders were accepted. Then the way to fortune lay open before them. They opened quarries on their own land, where they found an inexhaustible supply of stones easily broken to the required size. With suitable stone ready to their hands they had a great advantage over all rivals, and for a generation the macadamising of the roads in the neighbourhood was practically a monopoly in the Brontë family.

I remember the excellent carts and horses

employed by the Brontës on the roads, and I also distinctly recollect that the names painted on the carts were spelled "Brontĕ," the pronunciation

THE BRONTË HOME.

being "Brunty," never "Prunty," as has been alleged.

With the lucrative monopoly of road-making, added to their farm profits, the Brontës grew in wealth. They raised on their farm the oats and fodder required by the horses; and as the brothers did a large amount of the work themselves, and had nothing to purchase, the money received for road-making was nearly all profit.

In those days the Brontës added field to field, until they owned a considerable tract of land, which they held from a model landlord called Sharman. That was the period at which the two-storied house, shown in the picture, was built ; and there were other houses occupied by the Brontës from the two-storied house down to the thatched cottage. In fact, the house of Red Paddy McClory, in which Alice was born and reared, stood about half-way between the two-storied house and a cabin a little to the south of it. The foundations of the house in which Charlotte Brontë's Irish grandmother was born are still visible.

Shortly after the death of old Hugh, and in the time of the Brontë prosperity, one of the brothers, called Welsh, opened a public-house in the thatched cabin referred to, and from that moment, as far as I have been able to make out, the tide of the Brontës' prosperity turned.

Everything the Brontës did in those days was genuine. Their whiskey was as good in quality as their roads, and I fear it must be added that they were among the heartiest customers for their own commodities. They ceased to work on the roads, and their hard-earned money slipped through their fingers, and the public-house became the meeting-place for the fast and wild youth of the locality.

Then another brother, called William, but known

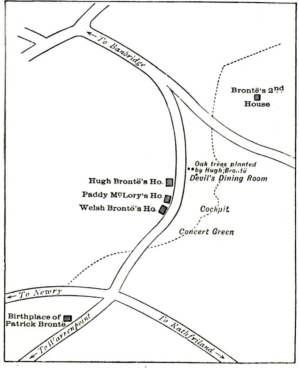

THE BRONTË HOMELAND.

as Billy, opened on the Knock Hill another public-house, which also became a centre of demoralisation to the young men of the district, and a source of

THE BRONTËS IN IRELAND

degradation to the keeper. I remember both these pests in full force. They were much frequented by Orangemen, who, when tired of playing "The Protestant Boys," used to slake their thirst and fire their hatred of the *Papishes* by drinking Brontë's whiskey.

In those days everybody drank. At births, at baptisms, at weddings, at wakes, at funerals, and in all the other leading incidents of life, intoxicating liquors were considered indispensable. If a man were too hot he drank, or if he were too cold he drank. He drank if he were in sorrow, and he drank when in joy. When his gains were great he drank, and he drank also when crushed by losses. The symbol of universal hospitality was the black bottle.

Ministers of the gospel used to visit their people quarterly. On those visitations the minister was accompanied by one of his deacons or elders. Into whatever house they entered they were immediately met by the hospitable bottle and two glasses, and they were always expected to fortify themselves with spirituous draughts before beginning their spiritual duties, and they did. As the visitors called at from twelve to twenty houses on their rounds, they must have been "unco' fu'" by the close of the day.

It is interesting to remember that when the drinking habits of the country were at their height,

THE DAILY ROUND

the temperance reformation was begun in Great Britain * by the best friend the Brontës had, the Rev. David McKee. It is of still greater interest, in our present investigation, to know that Mr McKee was moved to the action which has resulted in the great temperance reform, by the Brontë public-houses at his door, and by the demoralisation they were creating.

The little incident which has led to such momentous results came about in this way. The Rev. David McKee of Ballynaskeagh was the minister of the Presbyterian Church of Anaghlone. He had built his church, and he was largely independent of his congregation. One Sunday he thought fit to preach on the Rechabites. In the

---

* "Ireland spoke first, by the Rev. Dr. Edgar of Belfast, an able Presbyterian professor in the Theological College. He was visited in 1829 by the Rev. Joseph Penney, an Irish Presbyterian minister and old friend returned from America, who told him of what was doing there. This probably gave the start in Europe. But while Mr. Penney gave the actual start, Dr. Edgar had been prepared for it shortly before by the Rev. David McKee, a Presbyterian minister near Belfast, who preached a sermon on the Rechabites and drinking habits, which so disturbed his congregation that a crowd of them came to his house next morning requiring him to recant and apologise next Sunday. He replied by printing his sermon, which went far and wide, for his commanding talents were well known. He had taught both Edgar and Penney when boys."—*The Early History of the Temperance Movement, and the Practical Lessons it Teaches us*, by John M. Douglas, Esq., London.

126   *THE BRONTËS IN IRELAND*

sermon he ridiculed and denounced the drinking habits of the time. The sermon fell on the congregation like a thunderbolt from a cloudless sky. Blank amazement in the audience was succeeded by hot indignation.

On the following morning an angry deputation from the congregation waited on Mr. McKee. He listened to them with patient courtesy while they urged that the sermon should be immediately burnt, and that an apology should be tendered to the congregation on the following Sunday.

When the deputation had exhausted themselves and their subject, Mr. McKee began quietly to draw attention to the happy homes which had been desolated by whiskey, the brilliant young men whom it had ruined, the amiable neighbours whom it had hurried into drunkards' graves ; and then he pointed to the Brontës as an example of the baneful influence of the trade on the sellers of the stuff themselves.

The deputation, some of them Orangemen, were in no mood to listen to radical doctrines subversive of their time-honoured customs, and they began to threaten.

Mr. McKee, who was six feet four inches high, and of great muscular power, drew himself up to his full stature, and calling to his servant, then at breakfast in the kitchen, told him to saddle his best mare, as he wished to ride in haste to Newry

THE DAILY ROUND

to publish his sermon in time for circulation at church on the following Sunday. Then, turning to the deputation, he thanked them for their early visit, which he hoped would bear fruit, and bowed them out of his parlour.

He rode the best horse in the district, and he never drew rein till he reached the printing office in Newry, and he had the sermon ready for circulation on the following Sunday, and handed it himself to his people as they retired. Hundreds of thousands of copies have been since issued, and it is still in circulation.

In 1798 Mr. McKee, then a youth, watched from a hill in his father's land the battle of Ballynahinch. He had in his arms at the time a little nephew, who had been left in his charge. The little nephew became the famous Dr. Edgar of Belfast, who used to boast playfully that he was "up in arms" at the battle of Ballynahinch.

Mr. McKee sent a copy of *The Rechabites* to his eloquent nephew. Dr. Edgar read the sermon, and then rising from his seat proceeded swiftly to carry all the whiskey he had in the house into the street and empty it into the gutter. With that drink-offering Dr. Edgar inaugurated the great temperance reform. From Ireland he passed to Scotland, and from Scotland to England. The whole kingdom was mightily stirred, and the temperance cause has ever since continued to flourish. The

128   *THE BRONTËS IN IRELAND*

little seed, stimulated at first by the Brontë public-houses, has become a great tree, the branches of which extend to all lands.

We have now seen the Brontës in the daily round of their common pursuits. In the next chapter we shall see old Hugh in the light of his Brontë genius.

CHAPTER XV

THE IRISH RACONTEUR, OR STORY-TELLER

THE *hakkawāti* is the Oriental story-teller, the man who, beyond all others, relieves the tedium and wearisomeness of Oriental life. I have often watched the Oriental *hakkawāti*, seated in the centre of a large crowd, weaving stories with subtle plots and startling surprises, using pathos and passion and pungent wit, and always interspersing his narratives with familiar incidents, and laying on local colour to give an appearance of *vraisemblance*, or reality, to the wildest fancies.

The Arabian *hakkawāti* generally tells his stories at night when the weird and wonderful are most effective. He has always a fire so arranged as to light up his countenance with a ruddy glow, so that the movements and contortions of a mobile face may add support to the narrative. He sometimes proceeds slowly, stumbling and correcting himself as Disraeli used to do, as if his one great desire were to stick to the literal truth.

Without any apparent effort to please, the

130 *THE BRONTËS IN IRELAND*

hakkawāti keeps his finger on the pulse of his audience. Should they show signs of weariness, he makes them smile by some pleasantry ; and as the Arab holds that smiles and tears are in the same *khurg*, or wallet, he brings something of great seriousness on the heels of the fun, and works himself into a white heat of passion over it, the veins rising like cords on his forehead and his whole frame convulsed and throbbing, the rapt audience following in full sympathy with every word.

I have seen the Arabs shivering and pale with terror as the *hakkawāti* narrated the fearful deeds of some imaginary *Jann* ; and I have seen them feeling for their daggers, and ready to spring to their feet, to avenge some dastard act of imaginary cruelty, and a few seconds after I have seen them melted to tears at the recital of some fanciful tale of woe. I never wearied of listening to the *hakkawāti*, or in watching the artlessness of his consummate art ; and I have always looked on him as the most interesting of all Orientals, a positive benefactor to his illiterate countrymen.

Hugh Brontë was an Irish *hakkawāti*, almost the last of an extinct race. I knew several men who had heard him when he was at his best. He would sit long winter nights in the logie-hole of his corn-kiln, in the Emdale cottage, telling stories to an audience of rapt listeners who thronged around

THE IRISH RACONTEUR, OR STORY-TELLER 131

him. Mrs. Brontë plied her knitting in the outer darkness of the kitchen, for there was no light except from the furnace of the kiln, which lighted up old Hugh's face as he *beeked* the kiln and told his yarns.

The Rev. W. McAllister, from whom I got most details as to Brontë's story-telling, had heard his father say that he spent a night in Brontë's kiln. Brontë's fame was then new. The place was crowded to suffocation. At that time he reserved a place near the fire for Mrs. Brontë, and Patrick, then a baby, was lying on the heap of seeds from which the fire was fed, with his eyes fixed on his father, and listening like the rest in breathless silence.

Hugh Brontë seems to have had the rare faculty of believing his own stories, even when they were purely imaginary ; and he would sometimes conjure up scenes so unearthly and awful that both he and his hearers were afraid to part company for the night. Frequently his neighbours could not face the darkness alone after one of Hugh's gruesome stories, and lay upon the *shelling* seeds till day dawned.

The farmers' sons of the whole neighbourhood used to gather round Brontë at night to hear his narratives, and he continued to manufacture stories of all descriptions as long as he lived.

I have always understood that Hugh Brontë's

stories, though sometimes rough in texture, and interspersed with emphatic expletives, after the manner of the time, had always a healthy, moral bearing. As a genuine Irishman, he never used an immodest word, or by gesture, phrase, or innuendo, suggested an impure thought. On this point all my informants were unanimous. He neither used unchaste words himself, nor permitted any one to do so in his house. Tyranny and cruelty of every kind he denounced fiercely. Faithlessness and deceit always met condign punishment in his romances ; and in cases where girls had been betrayed, either the ghost of the injured woman or the devil himself in some awful form wreaked unutterable vengeance on the betrayer.

Hugh Brontë was a moral teacher, and a power for good as far as his influence extended. There are still some old men living in his neighbourhood who never understood him, and who are disposed to think he was in league with the devil.

It is always at his peril that any man dares to live before his time, or to leave the beaten track of the commonplace. The reformers have all without exception been mad, or worse, in the eyes of dull conservatism. Brontë dared to teach his neighbours by allowing them to see as well as hear, and those who were too stupid to understand were clever enough to denounce. By a very great

THE IRISH RACONTEUR, OR STORY-TELLER 133

effort Hugh Brontë learned to read late in life. He began at Mount Pleasant, with no higher aim than that of being able to write letters to Alice McClory when he could no longer visit her. He made rapid strides in learning under the tutelage of his master's children when he lived in Loughorne, and when he went to live in Emdale he knew the sweetness and solace of a few good books ; and he had always a book on his knee, which he read by the light of the kiln fire when he was alone. He knew the Bible, the *Pilgrim's Progress*, and Burns's poems well. Those were bookless days. The newspaper had not yet found its way to the people, and in a neighbourhood of mental stagnation it was something to have one man who could hold the mirror up to nature and lead his illiterate visitors into enchanted ground.

Many of Hugh's stories were far removed from the region of romance ; but he had the literary art of giving an artistic touch to everything he said, which added a charm to the narration independent of the facts which he narrated. The story of his early life which I have tried to reduce to simple prose was delivered in the rhapsodic style of the ancient bards, but simple enough to be understood by the most unlettered plough-boy. And I have always understood that none of Brontë's stories were so acceptable as the plain record of his early hardships.

134   *THE BRONTËS IN IRELAND*

Mingled with all his stories shrewd maxims for life and conduct were interwoven; but in his oration on tenant-right he broke new ground, and showed that, under different circumstances, he might have been an advanced statesman, and saved his country from unutterable woe.

Hugh was superstitious, but while his superstitious character descended to all his children, the faculty of story-telling was inherited, as far as I have been able to ascertain, by Patrick alone. All the sons and daughters talked with a dash of genius; but I have never heard of any of them except Patrick trying to tell a story.

Patrick at the age of two or three used to lie on the warm *shelling* seeds, and listen to his father's entrancing stories as if he understood what was being said, and he seems to have caught something of his father's gift and power. Miss Nussey has often told me of Patrick's power to rivet the attention of his children, and awe them with realistic descriptions of simple scenes. All the girls used to sit in breathless silence, their prominent eyes starting out of their heads, while their father unfolded lurid scene after scene; but the greatest effect was produced on Emily, who seemed to be unconscious of everything else except her father's story, and sometimes the descriptions became so vivid, intense, and terrible, that they had to implore him to desist.

THE IRISH RACONTEUR, OR STORY-TELLER 135

Miss Nussey had opportunities for observing the Brontë girls that no other person had. She became Charlotte's friend at school when both were homesick and needed friends. She continued to be her fast friend through life. Gentle Annie Brontë died in her arms, and she was Charlotte's true consoler when the heroic Emily passed swiftly away. She early discovered the ring of genius in Charlotte's letters, and preserved every scrap of them, and it is chiefly through those letters that the Brontës are known in England. She was Charlotte's confidante in all private transactions and love matters, and she might have been a nearer friend still had Charlotte not refused an offer of marriage from her brother, an incident in the novelist's life here for the first time, I believe, made public.

Miss Nussey was not only Charlotte's devoted friend, but she was a constant visitor at Haworth, and a keen observer. She had a great power of discernment in literary matters, and a very considerable literary gift herself. She had not to wait till *Jane Eyre* and *Wuthering Heights* were published to learn that Charlotte and Emily were endowed with genius. We owe it to her penetrating sagacity that we know so much of the vicar's daughters. She watched their growth of intellect, and everything that ministered to it, and she believes firmly that the girls caught their inspiration from their

10

136　　THE BRONTËS IN IRELAND

father, and that Emily got not only her inspiration, but most of her facts from her father's narratives.*

"The dirty, ragged, black-haired child" brought home by Mr. Earnshaw from Liverpool is none other than the real dirty, naked, black-haired foundling discovered on the boat between Liverpool and Drogheda, and taken home by Charlotte's great-great-grandfather and great-great-grandmother to the banks of the Boyne. The artist, however, is not a mere copyist, and hence, while the story starts from

* Swinburne, in his *Note on Charlotte Brontë*, says: "Charlotte evidently never worked so well as when painting more or less directly from nature. . . . In most cases probably the design begun by means of the camera was transferred for completion to the canvas." In contrasting Charlotte with her sister, he says: "Emily Brontë, like William Blake, would probably have said, or at least presumably have felt, that such study after the model was to her impossible—an attempt but too certain to diminish her imaginative insight, and disable her creative hand." Surely the highest imaginative insight and deftest creative hand work from the model, nature, though the result may not be a mere portrait of the model!

No author has so narrowly missed understanding Emily Brontë's character as Miss A. Mary F. Robinson. In her book *Emily Brontë*, one of the "Eminent Women" Series, she declares that, "While the West Riding has known the prototype of nearly every person and nearly every place in *Jane Eyre* and *Shirley*, not a single character in *Wuthering Heights* ever climbed the hills round Haworth." Here Miss Robinson was on the way to the mystery, and she comes still nearer to it when she narrates how the Rev. Patrick Brontë used to "entertain the baby Emily with his Irish tales of violence and horror." She turned her back on

THE IRISH RACONTEUR, OR STORY-TELLER 137

existing facts and follows the general outline of the real, it is not the very image of the real, and makes deviations from the original facts to meet the exigencies of art.

There is no difficulty in recognising the original of the "incarnate fiend" Heathcliffe in the man Welsh who tormented Hugh Brontë, Patrick's father, in the old family home near Drogheda. Had Welsh never played the demon among the

the truth, however, when she gave currency to the silly theory that Emily, in *Wuthering Heights*, was simply making printer's copy of her brother's shame, "a chart of proportions by which to measure, and to which to refer, for correct investiture, the inspired idea." Nor was Miss Robinson altogether innocent in placing such a stigma on the memory of Emily Brontë, for she writes, "Emily cared more for fairy tales, wild, unnatural, strange fancies, suggested, no doubt, in some degree by her father's weird Irish stories. . . . Mr. Brontë loved to relate fearful stories of superstitious Ireland, or barbarous legends of the rough dwellers in the moors. . . . Emily, familiar with all the wild stories of Haworth for a century back, and nursed on grisly Irish horrors, tales of 1798, tales of oppression and misery,—Emily, with all this eerie lore at her finger-ends, would have the less difficulty in combining and working the separate motives into a consistent whole." It is a pity that an excellently written book has been vitiated by an unworthy hypothesis. Miss Nussey, from whom Miss Robinson got most of her information, gave no countenance to her theory. Emily Brontë never looked on her brother with a frown. The more commonplace Charlotte sulked and complained; but no word of reproach ever passed Emily's lips, and no power in the universe could have drawn from her one syllable of censure for thoughtless gossip to work upon.

Brontës, Emily Brontë had never placed on canvas Heathcliffe, "child neither of Lascar nor gipsy, but a man's shape animated by demon life—a ghoul, an afreet."

Nelly Dean, the benevolent but irresolute medium of romance and tragedy, is Hugh's Aunt Mary, clear-eyed as to right and duty, but ever slipping down before the force of circumstances. And old Gallagher on the banks of the Boyne, with the "Blessed Virgin and all the saints" on his side, is none other than the original of the old hypocrite Joseph. Gallagher is Joseph speaking the Yorkshire dialect.

And Edgar Linton is the gentle and forgiving brother of Alice, our friend Red Paddy McClory, who took his sister home after her runaway marriage with a Protestant, and finally took the whole Brontë family under his roof and gave them all he possessed. Even Isabella Linton's flight and marriage had solid foundation in fact, either in Alice Brontë's romantic elopement with Hugh, or in the more tragic circumstances of Mary Brontë's marriage with Welsh.

It is not credible, I again assert, that Patrick Brontë in his story-telling moods never narrated to his listening daughters the romance of their grandfather and grandmother. It is true Miss Nussey never heard any reference to the story, nor did the Brontës ever in her presence refer to

THE IRISH RACONTEUR, OR STORY-TELLER 139

their Irish home or friends or history, though at the very time she was visiting Haworth they were in constant communication with their Irish relatives, and, as we shall see, one of the uncles actually visited them as Charlotte's champion, and one of them had visited Haworth at an earlier date.

The Brontës were too proud to talk even to their most intimate friends of their Irish home, much less to expose the foibles of their immediate ancestors to phlegmatic English ears ; but Patrick Brontë would not omit to tell his daughters the thrilling adventures of their ancestors ; and the girls, having brooded over the incidents, reproduced them in variant forms, and in the sombre setting of their own surroundings.

The originals lived and died, acted and were acted upon in Louth and Down ; but on the steeps of *Wuthering Heights* they strut again, speaking with the Yorkshire brogue and braced by the tonic air of the northern downs. None of the stories betray their origin so clearly as *Wuthering Heights*, just as, none of the novelists were so fascinated with their father's tales as Emily. But the stories are all Brontë stories, an echo of the thrilling narratives related by old Hugh, and retold to his children, I believe, a hundred times by Patrick.

Of course all the stories are made to live again

under new forms, each writer giving the stamp of her own character to the new creations, and each adding the necessary rouge which fiction requires to make up for fact. Artists of the Brontë stamp are not portrait painters nor mere reproducers. They never were content to be mere lackeys of nature. They were above nature, and everything without and within themselves they placed under contribution.

Even the rough and rugged characters that have come from the hands of Emily show the work of the artist. She added to the repulsive Heathcliffe qualities of her own. She is perfectly serious when she puts into Lockwood's mouth the following words : " Possibly, some people might suspect him (Heathcliffe) of a degree of underbred pride. I have a sympathetic chord within that tells me it is nothing of the sort. I know, by instinct, his reserve springs from an aversion to showy displays of feeling,—to manifestations of mutual kindliness. He'll love and hate equally under cover, and esteem it a species of impertinence to be loved or hated again. No : I'm running on too fast ; I bestow my own attributes over liberally on him."

Knowing the model from which Emily Brontë worked, there are few passages that throw more light on. the artist than this.

Catherine Linton was modelled on the lovely Alice McClory, who bequeathed to her clever

THE IRISH RACONTEUR, OR STORY-TELLER 141

granddaughters all the personal attractions they possessed ; but here again Emily bestows attributes of herself and sisters on her stately and lily-like grandmother :—

"She (Catherine) was slender, and apparently scarcely past girlhood : an admirable form, and the most exquisite little face that I have ever had the pleasure of beholding ; small features, very fair ; flaxen ringlets, or rather golden, hanging loose on her delicate neck ; and eyes, had they been agreeable in expression, that would have been irresistible."

The picture is neither that of a Brontë of the Haworth vicarage, nor is it a portraiture of the flower plucked in Ballynaskeagh by Hugh Brontë ; but it is Alice McClory diluted with an infusion of the Penzance Branwells, and the effect is a perfect and beautiful picture, more pleasing indeed than a lifelike portrait with all the radiant beauty of the charming Alice when she rode off to Magherally Church with the dashing Hugh Brontë.

CHAPTER XVI

HUGH BRONTË AS A TENANT-RIGHTER

HUGH BRONTË worked up to his tenant-right doctrines by a series of assertions, negative and positive, on religious, political, and economic questions. His address in which he set forth his views on such matters, approximated to the form of a lecture more nearly than any of his other talks, which were generally in the narrative form. The following are the chief points of the discourse as given to me by my old tutor and friend, and the propositions were never varied, except in the mere wording, although the statement had never, I believe, except by myself, been formally written out.

Hugh Brontë always began with a little black Bible in his hand or on his knee, and his first negative assertion was :—

I. THE CHURCH IS NOT CHRIST'S.

Laying his hand on the little book he would declare that he found grace in the Bible, but in the Church only greed. Once, and only once, he had appealed to a parson. He was hungry, naked,

HUGH BRONTË AS A TENANT-RIGHTER 143

and bleeding ; but the great double-chinned, red-faced man had looked on him as if he were a rat, and without hearing his story had him driven off by a grand-looking servant in livery, who cracked a whip over his head and swore at him.

In Hugh Brontë's eyes the parsons got their livings for political services, and not for learning or goodness. Enormous sums were paid to them to do work that they did not do. They rarely visited their parishes, and their duties were performed by hungry and ill-paid curates. When they did return occasionally to their livings, they were heard of at banquets, where they ate and drank too freely, and at other resorts, where they gambled recklessly. They were seen riding over the country after foxes and hounds, and sitting in judgment on the men whose grain they had trampled down, and sending them to penal servitude for trapping hares in their own gardens. They were said to be ignorant, but they were known to be immoral, irreligious, arrogant, and cruel. They acted as the ministers of the gentry, before whom they were very humble ; and they utterly despised the people who paid for their luxuries and supported their own priests besides.

They gave the sanction of the Church to violence, craft, and crime in high places, and they were as far removed as men could be, in origin, position, and practice, from the Apostles of the

New Testament. And yet, he added, they claimed in the most haughty manner that they, and they alone, were the successors of the Apostles, although they showed no signs of apostolic spirituality or apostolic service.

Hugh Brontë declared that he could not submit to the Protestant parson who despised him because he was poor, and could not aid in his promotion ; nor could he yield obedience to the Catholic priest who demanded utter subjection and prostration of both body and mind, and enforced his Church's claims by a stout stick. With these views it is not to be wondered at that Hugh Brontë did not belong to any Church.

To us now, who know the high character of the Irish clergy, his statements appear exaggerated and sweeping ; but it must be remembered that he spoke of them generally, in the closing decades of the last century. He expressed himself fiercely regarding the parsons, and in return they dubbed him atheist.

His second negative assertion was :—

II. THE WORLD IS NOT GOD'S.

He knew from the Bible that God had made all things very good, and that He loved the world ; but he held that a number of people had got in between God and His world and made it very bad and hateful. They were known as kings and emperors and rulers, and they had seized on the world by fraud and force. They lived on the best of everything that the land produced, and when they disagreed among themselves they sent their people to kill each other on their account, while they sat at home in peace and luxury.

These usurpers not only held sway over the possessions and lives of men, but they decreed the very thoughts men were to entertain concerning God, and the exact words they were to speak regarding Him, and when men presumed to obey God rather than men they were tied to stakes and burnt to death as blasphemers. For such sentiments as these Hugh Brontë was denounced as a socialist, a very bad and dangerous name at the beginning of the present century.

His third negative proposition was :—

III. IRELAND IS NOT THE KING'S.

He understood that King George III. was not a wise man, but that he was a humane man. Ireland was not governed by King George III., but by a gang of rapacious brigands. They constantly invoked the King's name, but only to serve more fully their own selfish ends. By the King's authority they carried out their policy of systematic outrage, until he hated the very name of the King whom he always wished to love.

The chief business of the King's representatives was to plunder His Majesty's poorer subjects. For this purpose the country was parcelled out, and

divided among a number of base and greedy
adventurers in return for odious services. Each
of these adventurers became petty king, or landlord,
in his own district, and lived on the wretched
natives. Every meskin of butter made on the
farm, every pig reared in the cabin, every egg laid
by the hens that roosted in the kitchen went to
support the landlord-king.

The cottages were mud hovels; the land was
bog and barren waste; the men and women were
in rags; the children were hungry, pinched, and
barefooted. But the landlord carried off everything except the potato crop, which was barely
sufficient to sustain life.

The landlord was a very great man. He lived
in London near the King in more than royal
splendour, or he passed his time in some of the
great cities of Europe, spending as much on gay
women as would have clothed and fed all the
starving children on his estate.

In English society his pleasantries were said to
be most entertaining regarding the poverty, misery,
and squalor of his tenants whom he fleeced; but
he took care never to come near them, lest his fine
sensibilities should be shocked at their condition.
His serious occupation was the making of laws to
increase his own power for rapacity, and to take
away from the people every vestige of right that
they might have inherited.

HUGH BRONTË AS A TENANT-RIGHTER 147

"The landlord takes everything, and gives nothing," was Hugh Brontë's simple form of the fine modern phrase regarding landlords' privileges and duties.

Hugh Brontë maintained that the landlord was a courteous gentleman, graced with polished manners, and that if he had lived among his people he might in time have developed a heart. At least, he could hardly have kept up a gentlemanly indifference in the presence of squalor and misery.

But he kept quite out of sight of his tenantry, or he could hardly have made so much merriment about the pig which was being brought up among the children to pay for his degrading extravagances.

The landlord's place among the people was taken by an agent, an attorney, and a sub-agent. The agent was a local potentate whose will was law; the attorney's business was to make the law square with the agent's acts; and the under-agent was employed to do mean and vile and inhuman acts that neither the agent nor the attorney could conveniently do.

The duty of the three was to find out by public inspection and by private espionage the uttermost farthing the tenants could pay, and extract it from them legally. In getting the landlord's rent each got as much as he could for himself. The key of the situation was the word "eviction." Then Hugh told the story of his ancestors' farm.

THE BRONTËS IN IRELAND

The Brontës had occupied a piece of forfeited land, with well-defined obligations to a chief or landlord. Soon the landlord succeeded in removing all legal restraints which in any way interfered with his absolute control of the place. Remonstrance and entreaty were alike unavailing. The alterations in title were made by the authority of George III., by the grace of God King of England, etc.

Hugh's grandfather drained the bog and improved the land at enormous expense. Every improvement was followed by a rise in the rent. His grandfather built a fine house on the land by money made in dealing, and again the rent was raised on the increased value given to the place by the tenant's improvements. Then the vilest creature in human form having ingratiated himself with the agent by vile services, the place was handed over to him, without one farthing of compensation to the heirs of the man whose labour had made the place of value. All these things were done in the name of George III., though the King had no more to do with the nefarious transactions than the child unborn.

From this conclusion Hugh Brontë proceeded to his fourth negative proposition :—

IV. IRISH LAW IS NOT JUSTICE.

He expressed regret that he was unable to respect the laws of the country. According to

HUGH BRONTË AS A TENANT-RIGHTER 149

his views the laws were made by an assembly of landlords purely and solely to serve their own rapacious desires, and not in accordance with any dictates of right and wrong. As soon might the lambs respect the laws of the wolves as the people of Ireland respect the laws of the landlords.

From this point he naturally arrived at his fifth negative proposition :—

V. OBEDIENCE TO LAW IS NOT A DUTY.

He said it might be prudent to obey a bad law cruelly administered, because disobedience might entail inconvenient consequences ; but there was no moral obligation impelling a man to obey a law which outraged decency, and against which every righteous and generous instinct revolted. Human laws should be the reflection of Divine laws ; but the landlord-made laws of Ireland had neither the approval of honest men nor the sanction of Divine justice.

Hugh's sixth and last negative proposition was :—

VI. PATRIOTISM IS NOT A VIRTUE.

He held that every man should love his country, and that every Irishman did ; but he could not do violence to the most sacred instincts of his nature by any zeal to uphold a system of government which dealt with Ireland as the legitimate prey of plunderers.

In other lands men were patriotic because they

150 *THE BRONTËS IN IRELAND*

loved their country. He loved his country too well to be a patriot. Love of country more than any other passion had prompted to the purest patriotism ; but who would do heroic acts to maintain a swarm of harpies to pollute and lacerate his country? who would have his zeal aglow to maintain the desolators of his native land?

Hugh Brontë gave out his views with a warmth that betrayed animus arising from personal injury. He was therefore declared to be disloyal, and that at a time when there was danger in disloyalty.

About the time Hugh Brontë was enunciating these sentiments the rising of the United Irishmen took place, and the pitched battle of Ballynahinch was fought in 1798.

It has always seemed to me strange that he should have passed through those times in peace, for the "Welsh Horse" devastated the country far and wide after the battle, and hundreds of innocent people were shot down like dogs. Besides, William, his second son, was a United Irishman and present at the battle of Ballynahinch. After the battle he was pursued by cavalry, who fired at him repeatedly, but he led them into a bog and escaped.

Hugh Brontë lived in a secluded glen ; but the "Welsh Horse" visited his house, and after a short parley with his wife, in which neither understood the other, one of the soldiers struck a light into

HUGH BRONTË AS A TENANT-RIGHTER 151

the thatch. Hugh suddenly appeared, and spoke to the Welsh soldiers in Irish, which it was supposed they understood as being akin to their own language, and they joined heartily with him in extinguishing the flames. They joined still more heartily with Hugh in disposing of his stock of whiskey. The inability of Hugh's neighbours to communicate with the Welsh may account for the fact that a man well known for such advanced and disloyal views passed safely through those troublous times.

Having completed his negative assertions or paradoxes, Hugh Brontë proceeded to state his theories, or positive conclusions. He laid it down as an axiom that justice must be at the root of all good government, and he declared emphatically, what O'Connell and agent Townsend have since maintained, that the Irish were the most justice-loving people in the world. He also held that unjust laws were the fruitful source of nearly all the turbulence and crime in Ireland.

Justice, he said, was nothing very grand. It meant simply that every man should have his own by legal right. This definition brought him to his tenant-right theory. In illustration he returned to the story of his ancestral home and the wrongs of his ancestors. He maintained that when his forefathers drained the bog and improved the land, they were entitled to every ounce of improvement

THE BRONTËS IN IRELAND

they had made. The landlord had done nothing for the land. He never went near it, and had never spent one farthing upon it; and he should not have been entitled to confiscate to his own profit the additional value given it by the labour of others.

He further declared that a just and wise legislation should secure to every man, high and low, the fruits of his own labour; and he maintained that such simple natural justice would produce confidence in Ireland, and that confidence would beget content and industry, and that a contented and industrious people would soon learn to love both King and country, and make Ireland happy and England strong. Just laws would silence the agitator and the blunderbuss, and range the people on the side of the rulers.

Hugh Brontë preached his revolutionary doctrine of simple justice in the cheerless east wind; but a little seed, carried I know not how, took root in genial soil, and the revolutionary doctrine of "*Every man his own*," at which the political parsons used to cry "Anathema" and the short-sighted politicians used to shout "Confiscation," has become one of the commonplaces of the modern reformation programme of fair play.

The doctrine of common honesty enunciated by Hugh Brontë has lately received the approval of

Liberal and Conservative governments in what **is** known as " Tenant-right," or the " Ulster Custom."

And here it is interesting to note that Hugh Brontë was a tenant on the estate which came into the possession of Sharman Crawford,*a landlord who first took up the cause of Irish tenant-right, and after spending a long life in its advocacy bequeathed its defence to his sons and daughters.

The Crawfords, like the Johnsons and Sharmans, their predecessors in title, were never absentee-landlords, and as men of high Christian character they always took a personal interest in their tenants, and would not, I believe, have failed to note any special intellectual activity among them. It is certain, moreover, that the Sharman Craw-fords, father and son in succession, spent their lives largely in the propagation of Hugh Brontë's views, both in the House of Commons and throughout the country ; and it seems to me not only probable and possible, but morally certain, that Brontë's

---

* I knew the late W. Sharman Crawford, M.P., well ; and I once talked with him of Hugh Brontë's tenant-right theories, of which he was thoroughly aware. I did not ask him if his father had got his views from Brontë, as I had no doubt of the fact. Miss M. Sharman Crawford writes me : " My father certainly originated tenant-right as a public question, though no doubt, long before the period when he strove to amend the position of Irish tenants, many thoughtful minds like his must have protested against the legalised injustice to which they were subject."

THE BRONTËS IN IRELAND

eloquent and passionate arguments dropped into the justice-loving minds of the Crawfords, and were the primary seeds of the great agrarian harvest which, on the lines of equity and with the full sanction of the legislature, is now being reaped by the tenant farmers in Ireland.*

Great results have thus flowed from the inhuman treatment of a child. Had little Brontë been left in the luxury of his father's home, it is not likely he would ever have been shaken up to original and independent thought; but the iron of cruel wrong had entered into his soul, and he felt that all was not well. He owed no gratitude to the existing order of things, and had no compunction in denouncing it; and having thought out and formulated a new

---

* In 1833 W. Sharman Crawford published a pamphlet embodying Hugh Brontë's doctrines, and making additional suggestions for the good government of Ireland. The pamphlet was republished by Dr. W. H. Dodd, Q.C., in 1892. Sergeant Dodd is an old pupil of the Ballynaskeagh school. He received his early education from Mr. McKee, the friend of the Brontës, and he was acquainted as a student with Charlotte Brontë's uncles. The following is his summary of the political portion of the pamphlet :—

" Mr. Crawford anticipates, as the probable result of refusing self-government to Ireland, the growth of secret societies, the influence of agitation, and the necessity of resorting to force in the government of the country. He touches upon the question of private bill legislation, of a reform of the grand jury system of county government.

" He points out that the creation of county councils without having a central body to control them is not desirable. And

theory, he proclaimed it with the strong conviction of an apostle who sees salvation in his gospel alone.

The daring character of Hugh Brontë's speculations in their paradoxical form, combined with the fierce energy of his manner in making them, secured for him an audience and an amount of consideration to which as an uneducated working man he could have had no claims. Indeed, Hugh Brontë's revolutionary doctrines were known far beyond his own immediate neighbourhood; and while many said he was mad, some declared that he only saw a little clearer than his contemporaries.

he suggests the creation of a local legislature for Irish affairs, combined with representat on in the Imperial Parliament, as the true method of preserving the Union, as the surest bond of the connection between the two countries, and as essentially necessary to tranquillity in Ireland.

"He refers, among other measures, to the disestablishment of the Irish Church, and the reform of the relations between landlord and tenant as being pressing.

"The arguments against his views are met and answered. One would think he had read some of the speeches lately delivered, so apt is his reply.

"It is curious to note the length of time Ireland has had to wait for the reforms he thought urgent; and it is sad to reflect how much suffering has been endured, and how much blood has been shed, because the men of his time would not listen to his words."

CHAPTER XVII

THE BRONTË FAMILY : GENEALOGICAL

IT is desirable here, at the risk of repetition, to take a general survey of the Brontë family before proceeding to specific details regarding the different members.

Shortly after the events which in 1688 rendered the Boyne memorable, Hugh Brontë (1) the elder occupied, as we have already seen, a house and farm on the banks of that river. It is not improbable that he received his possession for imperial services rendered in those turbulent times.

As we have also already seen, disaster befell Brontë's children through the artifices of the foundling called Welsh, who had been brought up in the family. He was supposed to have murdered and robbed old Hugh, and he finally possessed himself of his farm and of his youngest daughter, Mary.

The rest of the family were scattered abroad and disappeared ; but a young Hugh (2), a son of one of the dispersed brothers, came to live with his aunt Mary and her husband Welsh, who had assumed the name of Brontë.

156

This young Hugh was the grandson of the Hugh Brontë whom we first met by the banks of the Boyne, and he became the grandfather of the famous novelists. He had a son, Hugh (3), "the Giant."

Hugh, having escaped from Welsh's bondage,

THE LAST OF THE BRONTËS AUNTS.

married Alice McClory of Ballynaskeagh, a Catholic beauty and a pure Celt. They were married in the parish church of Magherally in 1776.

Regarding Hugh's appearance, Alice Brontë, the last of his family, speaking to the Rev. J. B. Lusk only a few days before her death, said: "My father came originally from Drogheda. He was

158   *THE BRONTËS IN IRELAND*

not very tall, but *purty* stout; he was sandy-haired, and my mother fair-haired. He was very fond of his children, and worked to the last for them. My mother died after my father."

Hugh Brontë went to live with his bride in the little Emdale cottage, and there on the 17th of March, 1777, Patrick, who became the vicar of Haworth and father of the novelists, was born.

Mary Brontë outlived her husband Welsh, and in after-years visited her nephew Hugh in County Down. There is a tradition that she was a very beautiful woman at the time of her visit; but as she must have been old then, there may be a reference to her daughter, who accompanied her.

Alice, speaking of this visit, said: "She came to see him in Emdale. Tarrible purty she was. A shopkeeper in Rathfriland courted her. . . . After she went home he sent after her, but she would not take him."

The Emdale cottage is in the parish of Drumballyroney, and not in the parish of Aghaderg, as has always been incorrectly stated; but the part of the register in which Patrick's baptism was entered is lost.*

---

* The register of the parish has lately been discovered in Banbridge by the Rev. H. W. Lett of Loughbrickland. Originally there were two volumes, and they were sold as waste paper for a mere trifle. One of the volumes was bought for fourpence, and used to paper up soap, candles, and such

William, the second son of the family, was baptised on the 16th of March, 1779; Hugh, the third son, was baptised on the 27th of May, 1781; James, the fourth son, was baptised on the 3rd

PATRICK BRONTË.

of November, 1783; Welsh, the fifth son, was baptised on the 19th of February, 1786; Jane, the eldest daughter and sixth child, was baptised on the

things. The other document rescued by Mr. Lett contains the minutes of the vestry meetings of Drumballyroney from 1789 to 1828. The baptismal register is complete from 1779 to 1791, and contains the registration of six of Patrick Brontë's brothers and sisters.

1st of February, 1789; Mary, the second daughter and seventh child, was baptised on the 1st of May, 1791. The register containing the names of Patrick, Rose, Sarah, and Alice, the remainder of the family, was destroyed.

Of the ten children, Patrick, the eldest, was born in Emdale, in the parish of Drumballyroney; and Alice, the youngest, in Ballynaskeagh, in the parish of Aghaderg; and the remaining eight, four boys and four girls, were born in the house in Lisnacreevy.

The Brontë girls were tall, red-cheeked, fair-haired, with dark eyelashes, and very handsome. They were massive, strong-minded women; and, as they despised men in their own rank of life, only one of them got married. Mr. McCracken writes thus of them: " With regard to the sisters of Patrick Brontë, I have seen them all except the one that was married. The rest lived and died unmarried. They were fine, stalwart, good-looking women, with rather a masculine build and carriage. Their lives were unstained by a single blot. They were not ordinary women. They were essentially women of character, and I think men were perhaps a little afraid of them."

William, or, as he was called, Billy, was a United Irishman. The story of his adventures at the battle of Ballynahinch forms an interesting chapter, for which I regret I have no space here.

He kept late in life a *shebeen* on the Knock Hill. Many stories, probably the exaggerations of his enemies, are told of his powers in the use of strong language and strong drink. He is said to have occasionally cleared out his own stock, and then

CHARLOTTE BRONTË.

to have spent the next six months in repentance and close application to business. He finally retired from the public-house on the advice of Mr. McKee, and went and lived with a prosperous son in Ballyroney. He had six sons, all of whom got on well in life.

THE BRONTËS IN IRELAND

Jamie worked sometimes as a shoemaker, made single-soled boots, and was a great favourite with children. He visited Patrick at Haworth, where he spent some time. Alice, speaking of Jamie, said, "He took a hand at everything, and he was very smart and active with his tongue." When he returned from Haworth he said, "Charlotte is tarrible sharp and inquisitive."

"Hugh and Welsh," she said, "were great fiddlers, and very industrious. They made a great deal of money by macadamising roads."

Hugh, who was called the Giant, was a religious man in his youth ; but towards the close of his life he lost his faith and grew superstitious. He was said to be great in religious controversy.

Welsh was the most gentlemanly of the brothers. Late in life he set up a *shebeen* in the little house in Ballynaskeagh. He had two sons ; one of them was drowned and swept away by a water-spout flood when he was crossing the river Bann. The other son, brought up in the *shebeen*, became a drunkard, and after a swift career of debauchery, compared with which Branwell's vices sink into insignificance, the kindly earth covered the pestilent thing out of sight.

There are now in Ireland a number of the descendants of the Brontës, who are industrious, prosperous, and in every way most exemplary. There are two or three in a destitute condition.

CHAPTER XVIII

THE BRONTËS AL FRESCO

I PROCEED with this chapter in the first person, though the story came to me at second hand. My tutor narrated it to me in the words in which he had heard it from a young cousin of his, and I am able to give it almost in the same words, and in the form in which I wrote it out at the time.

The scene described does not, however, rest on the authority of Mr. McAllister or his friend alone, but on the testimony of all who knew the Brontës in their home life. Similar scenes have been described to me by old men whose memory extended back to matters in the last century ; and quite recently when visiting the place Mr. Ratcliffe pointed out the exact spot where he himself had witnessed the Brontës engaged in their amusements. The story is so characteristic that I give it *in extenso*, and with all details as I got it :—

"In 1812 I made," said McAllister's friend "my first great journey out into the big world accompanied by my elder brother. We were then very young. The nature of our business obliged us to go on foot, and the distance traversed was two or three miles.

"Our errand brought us into the midst of the Brontës; and as we had to remain there six or seven hours, we had an opportunity of seeing under various aspects that extraordinary and unique family whose genius came to be revealed a few years later by three little girls on English soil.

"We first saw a group of the Brontë brothers together. I think there were six of them, and they were marching in step across a field towards a level road. Their style of marching and their whole appearance arrested our attention. They were dressed alike in home-spun and home-knitted garments that fitted them closely, and showed off to perfection their large, lithe, and muscular forms. They were all tall men, but with their close-fitting apparel and erect bearing they appeared to be men of gigantic stature. They bounded lightly over all the fences that stood in their way, all springing from the ground and alighting together; and they continued to march in step without an apparent effort until they reached the public road, and then began in a businesslike way to settle conditions in preparation for a serious contest.

"A few men and boys watched the little group

THE BRONTËS AL FRESCO 165

of Brontës timorously from a distance ; but curiosity drew my brother and myself close up to where they were assembled. They did not seem to notice us, or know that we were present, but proceeded with a match of hurling a large metal ball along the road. The ball seemed to be about six pounds weight, and the one who made it roll farthest along the road was declared the winner.

" The contest was to them an earnest business. Every ounce of elastic force in the great muscular frames was called into action, and there was a profusion of strange strong language that literally made our flesh to creep and our hair to stand on end. The forms of expression which they used were as far from commonplace as anything ever written by the gifted nieces ; and as the uncles' lives were on a lower plane of civilisation, and their scant education had not reduced their tongues to the conventional forms of speech, they gave utterance to their thoughts with a pent-up and concentrated energy never equalled in rugged force by the novelists.

" We had never seen men like the Irish Brontës, and we had never heard language like theirs. The quaint conceptions, glowing thoughts, and ferocious epithets, that struggled for utterance at their unlettered lips, revealed the original quarry from which the vicar's daughters chiselled the stones for their artistic castle-building, and disclosed the original fountain from which they drew their pathos and passion. Similar fierce originality and power are felt to be present in everything produced by the English Brontës; but in their case the intensity of energy is held in check by the Branwell temperament, and kept under restraint by education and culture.

"The match over, and the sweepstakes secured, the brothers returned to their harvest labour as they went, clearing like greyhounds every fence that stood in their way. At that time no fame attached to the Brontë name, but the men that we had come upon were so different from the local gentry, farmers, flax-dressers, and such-like people who lived around them, that we became all at once deeply interested in them.

"From a distance we watched their shining sickles flashing among the golden grain, and caught snatches of songs which we afterwards found to be from Robert Burns. Our interest, however, in the Brontës was shared by no one. They were then neither prophets nor heroes in their own country, and they were regarded with a kind of superstitious dread by their neighbours rather than with interest or curiosity.

"Young as we then were, we persevered with our inquiries, and our curiosity was rewarded. We learnt that the Brontës had a brother, a clergyman in England, 'a fine gentleman,' then on a visit to

THE BRONTËS AL FRESCO 167

them, and that the Brontë family were in the habit of holding an open-air concert every favourable afternoon in a secluded glen below their house. I remember wondering if the clergyman ever broke out in the vigorous vernacular of his kith and kin ; but we were especially interested in the open-air concert.

" My brother and I by the nature of our errand could not return home till late in the evening, and as we were at leisure we made up our minds to assist at the concert. On pretence of gathering blackberries we explored the glen and discovered the place. No one would accompany us, and we were told with uneasy looks that it would be at our peril if we went to the concert, as the brothers had 'the black art,' and were all men to be avoided. We resolved, notwithstanding, to go as spectators, and waited with impatience till the day's work should be over.

" About six o'clock a horn was blown, and the reapers suddenly dropped their sickles and strolled down leisurely to the Concert Glen. We had already preceded them, and taken our places on a high ridge bordering on the Glen in a thicket of low brushwood.

" Three sisters were the first to arrive on the scene. They brought a spinning-wheel, a supply of oat-bread and buttermilk, and a green satchel, which contained a violin. The men sat astride the trunk of a prostrate tree, and disposed of their afternoon collation in an incredibly short space of time, one wooden bowl, or noggin, supplying milk to each.

" Scarcely had the frugal meal been ended, when one of the brothers began to thrum the fiddle, and quick as lightning two of the sisters and the other brothers were whirling and spinning airily over the grass. The other sister was busily plying her spinning-wheel and watching the moving scene. In turns each of the sisters took her place at the wheel, and the one relieved instantly plunged into the mazes of the dance.

" The girls were tall like their brothers, and picturesque in their red tippets. Like their brothers, they were handsome and graceful. They were mature maidens, but they had not lost their elegant figures or their fresh red-and-white complexions. Their home-made dresses, though of plain woollen material and simply made, fitted them well, and were in perfect harmony with their rustic surroundings. Their hair hung in ringlets round their shoulders, and they moved with unconscious grace, whirling over the greensward as if they scarcely touched it, or mazing through a ' country dance,' or an ' eight point reel,' or waltzing round and round in a manner to make the onlooker giddy.

" There was nothing in the performance suggest-

THE BRONTË DANCING GREEN.

THE BRONTËS AL FRESCO

ive of the rough peasant or the country clown ; all was exquisite grace and courtesy. The musician was also relieved from time to time, each of the brothers taking his turn at the violin.

"The scene was of the most weird and romantic character. The place selected for the family dance was in a secluded widening of the Glen, down which flows a little stream that makes a murmuring noise as it tumbles over stones and among the roots of alder and willow. It was wide enough to give full scope for extended gallops, and sufficient for all the exigencies of Sir Roger de Coverley. The ground was thickly carpeted with grass, and surrounded by large trees with overhanging branches ; the trees were festooned with ivy and honeysuckle, sweet briar and wild roses overflowed the hedges in great profusion, and 'flowering Sally' in pink bunches fringed the brook.

"The sun was sinking in the west, throwing dark shadows down the sides of the Newry mountains, and shedding a pale glory on Slieve Donnard and the other lofty peaks of the Mourne Range. Close by stood the Knock Hill, generally sombre and unpicturesque ; but on that occasion it glowed in the parting rays. The little valley as it dipped downward opened out to the west, and through the opening the setting sun poured a rich flood of light on the animated group, mating each dancer with a long dark shadow, and apparently doubling the number of figures that tripped lightly over the grass.

"As the sun dropped behind . the ridge of Armagh the concert came to an end, after a long bout of Scotch jigs, in which two and two in a row danced opposite each other, chased by their tall unearthly shadows.

"The closing scene was a great effort of endurance, but none seemed to weary, and with a few skips into the air, the arms raised in curves above the head, and the fingers of the men being made to crack, all was still.

"There were four spectators of this wonderful family gathering : my brother and myself ; a goat that was quietly barking a tree beside us, and pausing occasionally to look at the frantic display ; and, on the other side of the valley from where we were, the clergyman brother, who walked to and fro, in solemn black, apparently in meditation, and taking no notice of the gleeful recreation of his brothers and sisters.

"There was no dawdling when the dance was over. Each of the brothers bowed with an air of gallantry to each of the sisters, and then one of the brothers caught up the spinning-wheel, and, poising it on his shoulder, strode up the homeward side of the Glen. All followed smartly, and disappeared in company with the sober figure in black.

THE BRONTËS AL FRESCO 173

"We slipped out of the bower, where we had sat entranced, and hurried homeward, with feelings of uncertainty as to the reality of things in the gathering darkness."

This is the most complete account I have ever heard of the summer evening concerts held by the Brontës. Others had often seen the same large-limbed, sinewy children of Anak dancing on the green with their flying shadows; but they had failed to appreciate the sylph-like motions of the maidens or the stately curvetting of the gigantic brothers, and looked on the whole exhibition as something uncanny, and as tending to confirm the popular belief that the Brontës had dealings with the powers of the nether world.

The unique forms and forceful language of the Brontës were lost on their commonplace neighbours, who looked on them as strange and dangerous people. In fact, they were not regarded with much favour by the people of the district, from whom they carefully held aloof; and the belief that they were in league with the devil received a certain amount of confirmation, as we shall see by-and-by.

When I first began to take an interest in the Brontës, I was admonished in a mysterious manner to have nothing to do with such people. I was advised to keep out of their way, lest I should hear their odious language; and it was even hinted that

THE BRONTËS IN IRELAND

they might, in some satanic way, do me bodily harm.

I am bound to say that matters in this respect have not altered much since for the better. My attempts recently to get accurate information on special points regarding the Brontës and their ways have been looked upon by some as a kind of craze, out of which, I have been assured, I was never likely to reap much credit. And even educated people, when replying to my inquiries on matters of fact, have sometimes felt called on to remind me that I was taking much pains with regard to a dangerous and outlandish family. In fact, the Brontës paid the usual penalty for being a little cleverer than the people with whom they came in contact and with whom they never associated.

The Brontës looked down on people in their own rank of life, and permitted no familiarities of any kind; and the only person who ever joined in their dances, as far as is known, was Farmer Burns. As they held aloof from everybody, they were only known by their strange language and odd ways. Imagination filled up the unknown, and gossip, as usual, made the most of every little circumstance. The fact that Mrs. Brontë had once been a Catholic prejudiced in no small degree the minds of Protestants against the children.

CHAPTER XIX

THE BRONTËS, THE DEVIL, AND THE POTATO BLIGHT

THE Concert Glen and romantic brook witnessed very different ceremonies from that just described. At one period an awful drama took the place of lissom glee, when Hugh Brontë, "the giant," in wild passion, sought to come into actual bodily conflict with the devil.

The potato blight fell as a crushing blow on the hopes of the Brontës, and proved the turning-point of their fortunes. They were growing in prosperity, and had enlarged their farm by the savings of many years. Through industry and frugality they had added field to field until their material success seemed to be assured; but while they were rejoicing in the position to which they had attained, the potato crop blackened and melted away before their eyes.

Ireland at that time had two kinds of tenant farmers. One resembled the drowsy Oriental, who basks in the sun, and seems content not to live but to exist. A few wizened olives, a little black

176   *THE BRONTËS IN IRELAND*

bread, and a very small quantity of rancid oil, suffice to maintain the existence of the lazy Oriental. In fact, no Oriental ever died of hunger, except in times of general famine. The maximum of indolent existence can be had in the East for the minimum of toil.

In Ireland a large number of people on the land simply existed in those days. They knew that if they drained or improved their farms, the landlords would raise their rents, so as to sweep away the entire profits arising from their improvements. They were well aware that any enlargement or brightening of their homesteads would cause the agent to scent superfluous money, and put on the screw, for a tenant would be more likely to make an effort to hold on to a comfortable house than to an uncomfortable one. Every staple of thatch put upon the leaky roof, or bucket of whitewash brushed into the sooty walls of the cabin, gave the landlord a new hold on the tenant, and supplied the agent with a new pretext for increasing the rent for his master, or securing a present for himself. And there were agents so kindly disposed towards the miserable tenants, that they preferred one pound as a present to themselves to two pounds added to the landlord's rent-roll.

Under these circumstances tenants of the indolent type did not drain their land or improve the appearance of their houses, and if they had

THE BRONTËS AND THE POTATO BLIGHT 177

thriving cattle they kept them concealed in remote fields when the agent was about ; and when they were obliged to meet either agent or landlord, they decked themselves out like Jebusites in ragged and squalid garments. It thus happened that landlords and land agents never saw the tenantry except in rags, and thus the tenants contrived to order themselves lowly and reverently to their betters.

The land of the thriftless brought forth potatoes in plenty. A little lime and dyke scourings mixed together sufficed for manure. The potato seed was planted on the lea-sod, and covered up in ridges four or five feet wide. The elaborate preparation for planting potatoes in drills was then unheard of. Cabbage plants were dibbled into the edges of the ridges, and the potatoes and cabbages grew together. Abundant supplies of *west-reds* and *yellow-legs* and *copper-duns*, with large savoy and drumhead cabbages, only needed to be dug and gathered to maintain existence.

Oats, following the potato crop, provided rough wholesome bread, and little rats of Kerry cows supplied milk. Great, stalwart men and women lived on potatoes three times a day, with bread and buttermilk and an occasional egg. Sometimes in the autumn a lean and venerable cow would be fed for a few weeks on the after-grass (flesh put on in a hurry being considered more tender), and then killed, salted, and hung up to the black balk

in the kitchen for family use. This *pièce de resistance* was almost the only meat ever known in the
homes of such people.

Two pigs fattened yearly on potatoes, and a
few lambs taken from the early clover, met the
demands of the landlord. The wool of the sheep,
spun and knitted and woven at home, supplied scant
but sufficient wardrobes. For fuel they had whins,
or furze, cut from the fences and turf from the
bogs. The fire was preserved by *raking* a half-
burnt turf every night in the ashes; but a coal
to light the fire was occasionally borrowed in the
morning from more provident neighbours, and
carried with a pair of tongs from house to house.
Matches were unknown in those days.

The men broke stones by the road sides on
warm days for pocket-money or tobacco, and the
women obtained their little extras by the produce
of their surplus eggs, which they carried to market
in little osier hand-baskets.

Existence in such homes flowed smoothly, one
year being exactly like another. The people had
no prospects, no hopes, no ambitions. They lived
from hand to mouth, and, while all went well,
the produce of each day was sufficient for their
simple wants. In their diurnal rounds they
gathered their *creels* of potatoes, and drove their
Kerry cows to the fields, golden with tufted rag-
weeds and purple with prickly thistles.

Such people seldom had their rents raised or their improvements confiscated, for the simple reason that they never made improvements, and never sought, through sustained effort, to better their condition. They had no margin beyond the bare necessaries of life, no resources to fall back upon in case of calamity. With barely enough to supply their daily wants and no more, they lived on the verge of starvation, and when the famine came they starved.

Such people were not ashamed to accept outdoor relief, or even to enter the most degrading of prisons, Irish workhouses; but to many of the thriftless poor the potato blight was a sentence of death. The feeble staff on which they leant was stricken from their hands, and they sank without a struggle, to rise no more.

The Brontës were people of a different fibre. They would not succumb without a struggle. They had advanced from the Emdale cabin to the Lisnacrеevy cottage, and thence to the house and farm in Ballynaskeagh. The primitive corn-kiln, with its insignificant and precarious profits, had been abandoned for the lucrative occupation of macadamising roads and cultivating the land.

The Brontës worked hard, and were frugal as well as industrious. They had hoarded the savings of many years, and invested all in a new farm, and they felt that they had a right to

180 *THE BRONTËS IN IRELAND*

look forward to a condition of prosperity and independence.

The class to which the Brontës belonged differed widely from the inert and feckless farmers that encumbered many a bankrupt estate. They did not live from hand to mouth, spending each day's efforts on each day's wants, and passing the summer in an easy doze. No people on earth slaved so hard as Irish tenant farmers. They worked late and early. Their wives and daughters and little children rose with the sun and laboured the livelong day. Every good thing raised on the farm went to market to meet the landlord's exactions and to add to the little store. Butter, bacon, fowl, eggs, and such-like, raised by the laborious housewife, were sacred to the landlord and to the hoards accumulated against the rainy day.

Such tenant farmers improved their lands and their houses, and consequently the landlords raised their rents in proportion to their improvements.

For such slaves there was little recreation except the half-holiday on Christmas Day, and the party displays on the 12th of July or the 17th of March. No toil, however, could crush out of them the desire to better their lot; but their moiling and slaving seldom resulted in anything more brilliant than a five-pound note to pay a son's passage to America, or a twenty-pound portion for a daughter when she passed from the dreary drudgery of her father's home to the abiding bondage of her husband's yoke.

The industry of the Brontës was not in vain. They lived under the best landlord that Ireland has ever produced. "The Sharman Estate," now known as the "Sharman Crawford Property," has always been blessed with a succession of Christian landlords, who have recognised that landed property has duties as well as privileges, and who have made it their life-work to propagate their doctrines by peaceful persuasion. Had Sharman Crawford been listened to in the House of Commons when he pleaded for the tenant farmers, there would have been no agrarian crime in Ireland ; but his was "a voice crying in the wilderness " ; he preached his gospel like "a linnet piping in the wind."

On the Sharman estate the Brontës had a fair field for their industries. They worked in absolute harmony as far as appeared to the outside world. They were a loving family, in their way, but without the shows of love. Their home was all the world to them, and they clung to it in early life, with something of the affectionate attachment that Emily Brontë and her sisters afterwards manifested towards the sombre parsonage at Haworth. They held aloof in a stoical manner from all neighbours, and neither sought nor accepted sympathy. They were healthful, hopeful, and happy in their farm, with the growing signs of plenty around them.

THE BRONTËS IN IRELAND

At this juncture the potato blight which cracked the framework of Ireland's economic arrangements blasted the Brontë paradise. The affection of the farmer towards his growing crops is in proportion to the solicitude with which he has watched over them; but the Brontës only learned fully what a treasure the potato crop had been to them when it was taken away. Never had their farm seemed so beautiful or the potatoes appeared so bountiful, but in a night the fields were smitten black, and the stench of rotting leaves filled the air. The tubers became rotten and repulsive instead of being white and floury.

Many theories were advanced to account for the calamity that had befallen the most important and indispensable product of the country. Pamphlets were published and sermons preached to show that national disaster had followed on the heels of national wrong-doing. Seasons for humiliation and fasting and prayer were set apart to supplicate Almighty God to take away the awful judgment.

The Brontë mind never ran smoothly with the common current. To them the evil appeared to be simply the work of the devil. The Brontës held the simple old Zoroastrian creed that everything beneficent was the work of God, and everything maleficent the work of the evil one.

Such opinions were not confined to the Brontës. As children we were given to understand that frosted blackberries were *clubbed* by the devil, who had blown his breath upon them as he passed by, and of course we all knew that the old enemy with the club foot lurked in the blackberry bushes.

Servants and common labourers held to the belief, no doubt prompted and fortified by the action of the Brontës, that the devil went bodily from potato field to potato field in his work of destruction ; and many reports got into circulation that he had been actually seen among the potatoes in the form of a black dog or black bull, but that he always vanished in a flash of lurid light when challenged.

I have very vivid recollections of the feelings of awe with which at night, when the wind moaned among the trees, I listened to these inflated stories, and also of the venturesome and prying scepticism with which I probed and pricked the bladders of superstition by day. No shadow of scepticism regarding the immediate cause of the blight ever crossed the minds of the Brontës, and so far as Hugh, the representative of the family, was concerned, he repaid the common foe by insult and scorn.

Hugh Brontë no more doubted that the devil in bodily form had destroyed the potato crop than he doubted his own existence. He saw the prop stricken from under the family by a malignant enemy, and he would not tamely submit to the personal injury. It was both cruel and unjust that the devil, who never did any work, should pollute the fruits of their toil. He would shame the fiend out of his foul work, and for this purpose he would go deliberately to the field and gather a basketful of rotten potatoes. These he would carry solemnly to the brink of the Glen, and standing on the edge of a precipice call on the fiend to behold his foul and filthy work, and then with great violence dash them down as a feast for the fetid destroyer. This ceremony of feasting the fiend on the proceeds of his own foul work was often repeated with fierce and desperate energy, and the "Devil's Dining-room" is still pointed out by the neighbours.

I knew a man who witnessed one of these scenes. He spoke of Hugh Brontë's address to the devil as being sublime in its ferocity. With bare, out-stretched arms, the veins in his neck and forehead standing out like hempen cords, and his voice choking with concentrated passion, he would apos-trophise Beelzebub as the bloated fly, and call on him to partake of the filthy repast he had provided. The address ended with wild, scornful laughter as Brontë hurled the rotten potatoes down the bank.

The dramatic power of the ceremony was so real, the spell of Brontë's earnestness was so con-tagious, that my informant, who was not a super-stitious man, declared that for a few seconds after Brontë's challenge was given, he watched in terror expecting the fiend to appear.

CHAPTER XX

THE MINOR AMUSEMENTS OF THE BRONTËS

IRELAND has always lacked the civilising and humanising influences of a common holiday. There is no day throughout the rolling year on which the people can meet as brethren, and no recurring seasons fraught with memories of good-will to all.

The two great holidays in Ireland fall on the 12th of July and the 17th of March. The 12th of July was celebrated by the Orangemen, not so much to do honour "to the glorious, pious, and immortal memory of William III.," who crossed the Boyne on that day, as to hurl defiance at their Catholic neighbours. St. Patrick's Day, the 17th of March, though kept in honour of a national saint whom Protestants and Catholics alike claim, had come to be regarded as a counter-blast to the Orange defiance, and in the minds of Orangemen generally was associated with disloyalty in politics and idolatry in religion.

The approach of these two great holidays was

signalised by the scouring of rusty old guns and pikes, and the casting of bullets and preparation of cartridges. The morning opened with the beating of drums and firing of guns. As the day wore on large bodies of men, decked out fantastically with orange sashes and orange lilies, or with green sashes and shamrocks, marched in procession to meet other processions at a given point, where fiery orations awaited them.

On such days there was a large consumption of spirituous liquors, or rather of fiery water. It was made up of vitriol, and blue-stone, and copperas, and other corrosive ingredients, and was flavoured with *potheen*. The beverage was prepared in great plenty and sold cheap.

Ordinary Irishmen are not, as a rule, either drinkers or drunkards. Drink has never yet come to be looked upon in Ireland as necessary food. Occasionally at fairs and markets Irishmen drink to excess, generally for good fellowship ; but when the drunken bout is over they become strict total abstainers till some circumstance calls them again to social hilarity.

To drink on the 12th of July and on St. Patrick's Day was part of the celebration. I can speak from personal observation of the 12th of July. To drink was to be loyal, and to drink deeply was to be a good Orangeman. The man who did not drink on the 12th of July exposed

THE MINOR AMUSEMENTS OF THE BRONTËS 187

himself to the suspicion of being little better than
a *Papish.*

There was no fastidiousness as to the stuff that
was drunk. The more pungent and fiery the
liquor, it was considered the more excellent and
palatable ; and I often witnessed the contortions
of countenance with which not only boys and girls,
but even strong men, swallowed the potations that
burnt down to the stomach and flushed up to the
brain.

The fiery orations were furnished by clergymen
who were supposed to be ministers of religion, and
the maddening drinks by the keepers of roadside
shebeens. An orange flag always floated on the
steeple of Rathfriland Episcopalian Church during
the whole month of July, and the *shebeen* windows
were ablaze with orange lilies throughout the same
month.

The processions on their homeward march had
many staggerers and stragglers. Their minds filled
with acrid eloquence, and their brains addled with
corrosive whiskey, the processionists became ex-
citable and quarrelsome, and when the common
enemy did not appear they often fought among
themselves. But sometimes the enemy did appear,
and then a pitched battle would ensue. Guns and
pistols blazed forth furiously all along the line of
march, but firearms in the hands of tipsy swaggerers
were more dangerous to friends than to foes.

188   *THE BRONTËS IN IRELAND*

With one solitary exception, and he was a McClory, I never knew any one killed or wounded in those noisy encounters except by his own weapon. The chief result of the party processions was an access of party hatred.

Orange and Catholic balls, held in country barns, were conducted on the same party lines, and, like the processions, created additional bad blood among neighbours. The elated revellers were sometimes attacked as they reeled homeward. In fact, the people saw each other only through the haze of party passion, and seldom came into sufficiently peaceful relations to discover that they were brothers. So much easier is it to fight for religion, than to live as Christians.

Even Christmas Day did not provide a common holiday on which the people might mingle peacefully together. To most of the Presbyterians the Christmas holiday appeared as a remnant of superstition. New Year's Day was kept as a holiday instead of Christmas Day by the Puritan party, but it was a sign of division rather than a bond of union.

Easter Sunday was a Catholic festival chiefly distinguished by the enormous quantities of eggs that were eaten on that day. But though the Protestants objected to the holiday, as being borrowed from the Church of Rome, they joined heartily in the general consumption of eggs. How-

THE MINOR AMUSEMENTS OF THE BRONTËS 189

ever poor the house, the table was heaped with boiled or fried eggs on Easter Sunday morning.

The Brontës, owing to their mixed origin, held aloof generally from the party demonstrations and squabbles that were so common around them. But on Christmas Day they organised a great yearly shooting match in the Glen. The prizes were game-cocks. Each of the competitors put down a penny. A small piece of paper was pasted on a barrel lid, which was propped up against a turf-stack, and whoever put most grains of shot into the paper was the winner.

A dozen game-cocks would be shot for and won, and then in the afternoon the same birds would be fought in the Cock-pit. I do not think there was much betting on the results of the contests. "They were fought for the fun of the thing," as a Brontë once said to me.

The Cock-pit, which was close to the "Devil's Dining-room," was well chosen to permit of a large number of people seeing what was going on. Cock-fighting was not merely a pastime resorted to on Christmas afternoon ; it became a passion with the Brontës in their decadence, and crowds often assembled round the Brontë Cock-pit on Sunday afternoons to watch the spirited little creatures destroying each other. In those days no particular disgrace seems to have attached to the cruel amusement which was very common.

THE BRONTËS IN IRELAND

Shooting matches were not limited by the Brontës to the great match on Christmas Day. They were the most common amusements of the Brontës. The brothers used to practise firing across the Glen at a mark fixed against a turf-stack throughout whole summer days, and weekly matches were got up with neighbours during the summer months.

The Rev. Patrick Brontë was said to be a good shot, and when on visits to Ireland he used to practise pistol firing for hours together, and when matches were on he always joined in them.

When he won prizes he always handed them over to be shot for again, and he also gave prizes to be competed for. He was passionately fond of shooting birds, and of practising with a pistol at a mark ; and I have no doubt that the pistol-firing at Haworth of which Mrs. Gaskell and others have made so much was a perfectly innocent trial of skill.

The Brontës had no equals in putting the "shoulder stone" and "drawing stone," and they were often engaged on summer evenings in hurling a metal ball along the road,—a practice that became so common and dangerous that the police got instructions to stop it.

In the times of the Brontës wakes might be considered as among country recreations. People from far and near thronged to the houses of mourn-

THE MINOR AMUSEMENTS OF THE BRONTËS 191

ing, and sat even in the room where the corpse was.
Clay pipes with long handles were handed round,
and abundance of tobacco ; but the chief attraction
was the unlimited supply of whiskey that was
served out. Any shortcomings in hospitality at
wakes were remembered for a generation.

Fighting was one of the minor amusements of
the Brontës. The fame of Welsh's great fight with
Sam Clarke covered the family with glory, and
other youths who were proud of their agility and
strength were anxious to try conclusions with the
stalwart brothers. It thus came to pass that they
were often drawn into scrapes in fairs and markets,
but they generally came off victorious.

An amusing incident occurred one day in Rathfriland fair. A man had offended Hugh Brontë,
and Hugh knocked him down. Soon the man's
son appeared on the scene, and hearing what had
befallen his father became greatly enraged. He
stripped off his outer garment as if for a fight,
and marched up and down the fair, waving his
arms in the most truculent manner, and shouting,
" Wher's the man that struck me faether ? "

When he had paraded the streets in triumph for
a while, Hugh Brontë stepped up to him and said,
" I'm the man that struck yer faether : what d'ye
want wi' me ? "

The furious person eyed Brontë deliberately for
a little, his ardour cooling during the pause, and

192 *THE BRONTËS IN IRELAND*

then he very meekly replied, " Heth, man, ye giv him a sevendable slap." And so the matter ended.

There was one pretty custom that the Brontës delighted in once a year—namely, the gathering of the may-flowers on May eve. On the last after-noon in April the brothers and sisters used to wander along the banks of the Glen, and gather the may-flowers that grew by the edge of the stream. On those occasions the sisters were decked out in the brightest colours at their disposal. The golden flowers were collected in posies and laid upon the greensward in the Glen, and then the brothers and sisters like fauns and satyrs danced around them. Towards the close of the dance they pelted each other with the flowers, and when night fell they gathered up all the bunches, and, bearing them home, scattered them on the roof of the house and around the door.

CHAPTER XXI

THE GREAT BRONTË BATTLE

THE fight between Welsh Brontë and Sam Clarke of Ballynaskeagh was an era-making event. The contest took place long before my time ; but I had a precise and full account of the battle from two eye-witnesses, John and James Todd. No encounter of the kind in County Down ever made such a noise or left such a lasting impression. Like the flight of Muhammed or the founding of Rome, it became a fixed point around which other events ranged themselves. It was a local Hĕjïra in the current calendar.

Women would speak of their children as born or their daughters married so many years before or after the fight, and old men in referring to their ages would tell how they had been present when Welsh Brontë licked Sam Clarke, and that they must have been of such an age at the time. It was one of those famous encounters which only required the pen of Pentaur to give it immortality in epic form.

The history of the affair, which I here submit,

embodies the conclusions at which I have arrived after comparing twenty or thirty versions; but I am specially indebted to the late Mr. John Todd of Croan, who was present at the battle with his brother James, and who narrated the incidents of the contest with many picturesque details. I should add, however, that the Todds were friends of the Brontës, and told the story with the warmth of partisans.

Welsh Brontë had a sweetheart called Peggy Campbell, and she had a little, delicate, deformed brother who used to go to Ballynafern school on crutches. Some of the big healthy boys thoughtlessly amused themselves by tormenting the little cripple. He often arrived home with his clothes torn and daubed with mud, and sometimes showing in his person the signs of ill-treatment. After the manner of schoolboys he would never "tell on" his tormentors. Welsh's sweetheart, however, had discovered the cowardly and cruel treatment to which her little brother had been subjected, and appealed to Welsh to protect him.

Welsh had, no doubt, often heard the story of his father's wrongs when a child, and at a hint from Peggy constituted himself the champion of the injured boy. He went to Sam Clarke, who was a near relative of the chief offenders, and begged him to interfere.

Clarke, who was said to be something of a

THE DUCKING POND.

THE GREAT BRONTË BATTLE 197

bully, advised Brontë to mind his own business, and Brontë replied that that was the exact thing he was doing; and then he added, as a threat, that unless Clarke restrained his brutal relatives he would chastise them himself. Hot words ensued, and Brontë and Clarke parted with expressions of mutual defiance.

Welsh Brontë's blood was up. His sense of justice was roused on behalf of an ill-used child, and his feelings of chivalry impelled him to become the champion of his sweetheart's brother.

Meanwhile the boys were meditating vengeance on their victim, who, in addition to the crime of meek endurance, had, they believed, proved a sneak and a *clashbeg* by telling of their misdeeds.

Welsh Brontë resolved to watch the children on their way home from school on the following day. He took up his position in a clump of trees somewhere near the Glen. He waited long, but the school-children did not appear, and, thinking that perhaps they had returned home by another path, he left his ambush to resume his work. Suddenly he heard hilarious cheering and piteous cries, and hurrying toward the spot whence the noise came, he found the school engaged in the ceremony of ducking the *clashbeg*, or talebearer.

They had taken the poor little cripple's crutches from him, and had placed him in the middle of a pond of water up to his neck, and then, having taken hands, they danced in a circle round the pond, chanting, "Clashbeg! clashbeg! clashbeg!"

Welsh Brontë took in the situation at a glance, and captured the two biggest Clarkes before they knew he was near. He then compelled them to wade into the pond and support their victim gently to the edge. When they had placed him on the dry ground he was so exhausted that he could neither stand nor support himself on his crutches, and Brontë obliged the Clarkes to carry him home on their backs, time about, the water dripping from their clothes. They did as Brontë directed them, but only after considerable chastisement.

The other children had fled home in alarm, and had given a highly coloured description of the inhuman manner in which Brontë was treating the Clarkes. Some of them reported that he had actually drowned them in the pond. On that night a challenge from Sam Clarke reached Welsh Brontë, and was instantly accepted.

The time for angry words had gone, and all preliminary formalities were carried out according to rule and with perfect courtesy. Seconds were appointed, and the day was fixed, and a professional pugilist, who resided at Newry, was engaged to act as referee. Both men went into close training, and the event was awaited with the most intense excitement for ten miles round.

The appointed time at last arrived, and it proved

THE GREAT BRONTË BATTLE 199

to be a charming summer day. A crowd number-
ing probably ten thousand, some estimated the
number at from thirty to fifty thousand, assembled.
They came together from Newry, Banbridge,
Rathfriland, Dromore, Hilltown, Warrenpoint,
Loughbrickland, and other country towns and
districts. Such an assemblage of the scoundrelism
of that region had never been drawn together
before. But they were not all scoundrels, for
public opinion had not at that time affixed the
stamp of infamy indelibly to the brutal exhibitions of the ring ; and it was said that a number
of sporting clergymen and country gentlemen were
present, undisguised and unashamed.

Many circumstances rendered the field famous.
The mothers of the combatants had fed their sons
for the fray like game-cocks. Oat-bread and new
milk were the staple food, which were supposed to
give muscle, strength, and endurance.

Shortly before the fight Clarke's mother, when
giving him his last meal before the encounter,
addressed him in the following words : " Sam,
my son, may you never get bit nor sup from me
more, if you do not lick the mongrel."

This Spartan speech spread like wildfire through
the field, and such was the code of honour on that
occasion that the exhortation was much blamed,
and led to a strong current of popularity in favour
of Brontë. The word " mongrel," referring to the

fact that her son's antagonist had a Catholic mother, was considered unfitting to be used in connection with the noble encounter that was about to take place. The words had wings, and flew over the whole field, and the spectators indignantly disapproved of them.

The ring was roped off in the hollow of a green field, and the multitude stood on the rising ground around, and all could see the entire ring. Three or four hundred men were enrolled as " special order preservers," and stood in a circle round the ring two or three deep. The seconds and referee and umpire were in their places at the opposite sides of the ring.

The hour fixed to begin was twelve o'clock, and prompt to the minute the two combatants strode down leisurely through the crowd, each with his sweetheart leaning on his arm. Their mothers already occupied seats of honour outside the ring.

Clarke was an older and maturer man than Brontë, and much bigger. Beside him Brontë, in his tight-fitting home-spun, looked slender and youthful and over-matched.

In consequence of the ungenerous and unguarded words spoken by Clarke's mother, sympathy, as we have seen, was already on Brontë's side, and this was greatly increased by the natural feeling that prompted the generous to take the weaker side.

THE GREAT BRONTË BATTLE 201

As far as I have been able to ascertain, the original cause of the quarrel was wholly lost sight of before the fight began. No one seemed to give a thought to the circumstance that Brontë had got into the affair by espousing the cause of a helpless boy. And, in this respect, did not the Brontë battle resemble most of our modern wars in which the rights and wrongs of the cause, and even the cause itself, are lost sight of in the strife? After listening to an account of the fight from some old man who had witnessed it, I have often asked what it was about; and I have generally got for answer, "Oh, it was just a fight," my question being evidently deemed irrelevant and somewhat silly. What was the cause of the Crimean war? It was just a war.

The champions stepped into the ring, and their sweethearts with them. As each stripped he handed his clothes to his future wife, and these two women stood, each with her lover's garments on her arm, till the matter was decided.

Time was not accurately kept, but the battle was said to have lasted three or four hours. At first Clarke had the advantage in strength and weight; but Brontë, who had long arms, was lithe and active and wiry, and did not seem to weary as the day wore on. On the contrary, Clarke began to show signs of fatigue; but the spectators thought he was simply husbanding his strength. Throughout the whole contest not a word was heard. Suddenly Miss Campbell's voice rang out clear in the silence, " Welsh, my boy, go in and avenge my brother, and the mongrel."

The minutes must have seemed hours to the girls, as they watched their future husbands struggling for victory on that summer day. Peggy Campbell, by her woman's instinct, discerned that the hour for the final effort and victory had come.

Welsh responded like a lightning flash. A few awful moments followed. The spectators held their breath, and some fainted, others covered their eyes with their hands or averted their faces. Terrific crushing and crashing blows resounded all over the field, and when the blows ceased to resound Sam Clarke was lying a motionless heap in the ring.

The crowd, after the long suspense and hushed silence, lost all control of themselves, and wanted to rush in and chair the victor ; but the special order preservers held the ring, and the sea of human beings surged against them in vain.

Welsh Brontë declined to receive congratulations until he had deposited his antagonist safely at home in bed. The fight was followed by no evil consequences, and Sam Clarke and Welsh Brontë became fast friends from that day forth.

From all accounts the fight seems to have been

a marvellous display of skill and endurance, very different from the sordid and brutal gambling contests patronised now by the roughs of all classes. Both of the combatants fought with the most chivalrous courtesy and utmost bravery, and the crowd awaited the result with imperturbable impartiality.

No word above a whisper had been heard during the long afternoon, till Brontë's sweetheart sang out her decisive commands, which in County Down rank with Wellington's " Up, guards, and at them ! "

All were agreed as to the closing scene. During the last few seconds the fight became so fierce and furious that the blood of the spectators ran cold. Nothing like it for wild fury and titanic ferocity had ever been witnessed by the crowd, and no such battle has ever since or before been fought in County Down.

The Rev. W. J. McCracken closes a vivid account of this battle with the following incident :—

" I can bear my personal testimony to the gratifying fact that Welsh Brontë lived to regret the fight. The only time I ever heard him refer to it was one day in my father's house. An old man chanced to come in who hadn't seen Welsh for a long time. He approached Brontë with a great ' How-do-ye-do?' adding, 'Och, Welsh, God be wi' the times when you licked Sam Clarke.'

THE BRONTËS IN IRELAND

The old flatterer evidently thought that Welsh would be hugely pleased ; but the only answer he gave him was in these words : 'All (pronounced *aa!*) folly, all folly, all folly ; but folk won't see their folly in time.'

"Brontë's answer, I remember, raised him a thousandfold in my esteem, while it snuffed out the old chap completely.

"Welsh Brontë was the perfection of manly beauty. Although an utterly uneducated man, he had the bearing and courtesy of a gentleman. In amiability and courtesy he was far in advance of any of his brothers, with whom I was acquainted.

"He had a strong, sensible way of putting a thing, and spoke in a low, kindly, pretty quick, and full voice." *

---

* The Rev. J. B. Lusk writes me that Mr. Frazer, now ninety-two years of age, was present at the encounter, eighty-two years ago. The meadow in which the affair took place belongs to the farm of Mr. John Barr of Ballynafern.

CHAPTER XXII

THE BRONTËS AND THE GHOSTS

THE Glen on the edge of which the Brontës lived lay secluded among hills, remote from the more frequented thoroughfares of the country. It was a beautiful and romantic spot by day, but lonesome and desolate at night. For miles round it had the reputation of being haunted, and few passed that way after dark. Those who were obliged to do so heard unnatural splashes in the stream, and rustlings among the bracken, and strange moanings and sobbings among the trees that swayed and tossed their branches, as if agitated by a hurricane when there was not a breath of air stirring. Strange and fitful cries were said to be heard in the Glen, and doleful wailings as of some one in agony.

Long ago, according to tradition, a woman had been murdered in the Glen by her false lover and betrayer. Hugh Brontë had told the story, with minute details and local colour, till everybody who frequented the gatherings at the Kiln knew it by heart.

The villain had enticed his victim to Rathfriland fair on pretence of getting the wedding ring. He had there attempted to strangle her, but she had escaped from his grasp, and was making her way home to her mother, through fields and by-ways, when, according to one of Patrick Brontë's unpublished songs.

> "Over hedges and ditches he took the near way,
> Until he got before her on that dismal day."

He waylaid her in the lonely Glen, and murdered her under circumstances of great atrocity. On that night the ghost of the murdered woman rushed upon the assassin, and with a wild scream dragged him from his bed, and through the window of his cabin, and down, down, down with unearthly yells to the bottomless pit. The whole story was told in rude ballad style, I believe, by Patrick Brontë, and sung to a sad air at local gatherings. The following is a verse :—

> "This young man he went to his bed, all in a dreadful fright,
> And Kitty's ghost appeared to him ; it was an awful sight :
> She clasped her arms (*a-rums*) round him saying, 'You're a false young man,
> But now I'll be avenged of you, so do the best you can.'"

The punishment was, according to local sentiment, well deserved ; but both were doomed to walk the earth for a thousand years. They had made their abode in the Glen, and hence the doleful and dismal voices that rendered night so fearsome in the neighbourhood of the Brontës.

Another circumstance added to the horror with which the Glen was regarded at night. It was said that, at a remote period, a man who had been robbed committed suicide at a crossing of the brook. He was still living when found with his throat cut, and up to his last breath he continued to moan, with a gurgling sound, "There were ten tenpennies in my pocket at the river." This story, told at night in a deep, guttural voice, each word long drawn out, and the last word pronounced *re-e-ever*, had a wonderful power of inspiring awe and making the blood run cold.

I believe the story was founded on fact. A man had committed suicide under the circumstances narrated, but in quite a different part of the country. The deed, however, had come to be located in the Brontë Glen, and increased the superstitious awe with which the place had come to be regarded. A snipe frequented the spot at night, and as people attempted to cross, it would start with a sudden screech from almost beneath their feet. The bird with the unearthly yell was supposed to be the spirit of the unfortunate man.

It was said that on one occasion Hugh Brontë was riding home with a neighbour. When they reached the Glen a headless horseman appeared on the road in front of them. The neighbour's horse stood shivering as if rooted to the ground ; but Brontë's horse, without any appearance of fear, walked up to the dreadful object, and Brontë, unmoved and without pause or word, simply cracked his whip at it, and it disappeared in a flash of light.

Ghost-baiting became a passion with the Brontës ; and though they were too proud to associate with their neighbours, they were not averse to being stared at and talked of by them.

The mill at the lower end of the Glen, where now stand Mr. Ratcliffe's dwelling-house and offices, was haunted. Lights flitted through it at night, and no one would go near it after sunset. When the terror was at its height Hugh Brontë armed himself with a sword and a Bible, and went alone to encounter the ghost, or devil, or whatever it might be.

The neighbours, who saw Brontë marching to his doom, stood afar off in the darkness and awaited the result. Unearthly noises were heard, and it was clear that a serious contest was proceeding. After a long delay Brontë returned, bruised and battered and greatly exhausted ; but he would give no account of what had transpired.

His secrecy regarding his adventure increased the terror of the superstitious, for it was given out and believed that Brontë, having been worsted in the encounter, saved himself by making some compact with the fiend or ghost ; and some even

THE BRONTËS AND THE GHOSTS   209

believed that he was ever after in league with the powers of darkness.

This awe-inspiring theory seemed to be confirmed by Hugh Brontë's subsequent action. One dark and dismal night the ghost in the Glen began to wail like a child in distress. The people barred their doors and covered their heads in bed with their blankets, and stopped their ears to keep out the unearthly sounds ; but Hugh Brontë went down quietly to the Glen and soothed the ghost, until by little and little its moaning died away. On several occasions it was believed that Hugh Brontë was actually seen in the Glen, standing with his hand on the mane of a magnificent black horse ; but when any neighbour drew near the black horse dwindled into a great black cat, which kept purring around Brontë and rubbing itself against his legs. As soon as the neighbour withdrew, the cat would again develop into the large black horse, and Brontë was often seen riding up and down upon it over precipices and ravines where there was no path.

There was also supposed to be a white-sheeted figure that used to frequent the Glen, carrying a little child in her arms. It was said that she was in the habit of asking for a night's lodging, but never seemed disposed to accept it. She generally kept her face covered or averted ; but when it was exposed it proved to be a toothless, grinning skull, with a light shining from each eyeless socket.

14

THE BRONTËS IN IRELAND

One of the Brontë sisters and her daughter lived in a house near by in which a man called Frazer had hanged himself. The house was declared to be haunted. Apparitions appeared in it both by day and night, but especially at night. Noises were heard, and rumblings in the rooms during the hours of darkness. When the inmates slept at night, something like a huge frog with claws used to rush up the clothes from the foot of the bed, and settle on their chests and almost suffocate them.

Hugh went to his sister's house one night, taking his gun with him. He upbraided Frazer's ghost for his ungallant and mean conduct in frightening lone women, and then called on him to come out like a man and face him. But nothing appeared, the ghost evidently declining to face a loaded musket. Brontë was importunate in his challenge, taunting the ghost with all kinds of sarcastic gibes and accusations, that he might irritate it into appearing ; but the ghost would not be drawn. Then he fired off his gun, and challenged the ghost to meet him face to face, using every scornful and reproachful epithet to drive it into a passion, but all in vain.

On the following night Hugh returned to the haunted house with a fiddle, and tried to coax the ghost to appear in. response to the music. The ghost, however, remained obdurate, regardless alike of threats, reproaches, and blandishments.

Brontë returned home that night in a state of

THE HAUNTED GLEN.

THE BRONTËS AND THE GHOSTS 213

wild excitement. All the way he incessantly called on Frazer to come and shake hands with him and make up their quarrel. He retired to bed in a delirium of frenzy, and during the night the ghost appeared to him and gave him a terrific squeeze, from which he never recovered. He died shortly after in great suffering, upbraiding Frazer for his heartless cruelty and cowardice, and he declared on dying that when he reached the land of shadows he would take measures to prevent Frazer from haunting his sister and niece. After Hugh's death the rumblings and apparitions ceased to trouble his sister's house any more.*

The great horror, however, of the haunted glen was the *headless horseman.* The phantom generally made its appearance among thickets of tangled bushes which no horse could penetrate, and glided silently over uneven and broken ground where no horse could have gone.

It always appeared to be ridden and guided by a man in flowing robes, whose feet were firmly in the stirrups, and whose hands held the bridle, but whose head had been chopped off, leaving only a red and jagged stump.

---

* Hugh Norton, now about ninety years of age, remembers the whole matter, and has given me both a verbal and written account of it. He says Hugh when dying gave orders that no whiskey should be served out at his wake, and threatened to return and destroy the company if his orders were disregarded.

THE BRONTËS IN IRELAND

The ghastly spectacle was so minutely described by the Brontës that others carried the picture of it in their imaginations, and it is not to be wondered at if many thought they saw the spectre among the shimmering shadows of the trees.

A neighbour of the Brontës, Kaly Nesbit, once gave to a number of us a vivid account of the apparition. He told the story with great earnestness, and with apparent conviction as to its truth. I give his account as nearly as I can in his own quaint language :—

"I heerd the horse nichering in the glen. It was not the voice of a horse, but of a fiend, for it came out of the bowels of the earth, and shook the hills and made the trees quake.

"Besides, there was no room for a horse on the steep bank and among the bushes and brablach. I had just had a drap of whiskey, about a naggin, and I wasn't a bit afeard of witch or warlock, ghost or divil, and so I stept into the Glen to see for myself whatever was to be seen. At first I could not see any inkling of a horse, but I heerd the branches swishing along his sides at the lower end of the Glen. Then I saw a large dark object, as big as a haystack, coming nixt me, and walking straight through trees and bushes, as if they were mere shadows.

"I juked down behind a hedge of broom, and as I hunkered in the shadow, he came on in the

THE BRONTËS AND THE GHOSTS

slightly dusk light. The horse was as big as four horses, and at a distance I thought the rider was a huge blackaviced man; but when he came fornenst me, the moon fell full upon him through a break in the trees, and then I saw that he was crulged up on the saddle, and that only a red stump stuck up between his shoulders where his head should have been.

"I escaped unseen, but just as the tarrible thing passed me it nichered again horribly, and I saw sparks of fire darting out of its mouth.

"It then turned and cut triangle across the valley, passing over the Cock-pit, and walking upon the air as it emerged into the moonlight. It walked up straight against the steep edge of the quarry-pit, and vanished into the bank. I saw it vanishing by degrees, like a shadow, at first black, then growing lighter and lighter till it entirely disappeared, and there was nothing on the high bank where it stopped but the bright moonlight."

Kaly Nesbit had the reputation of being a very good old man. I knew him pretty well, especially as a near relative of his had been my kind old nurse, who imparted to me much Brontë lore. I am sure he believed the fascinating story he told; but a "naggin" of whiskey is a rather indefinite quantity, and Kaly Nesbit on that night may have had his faculties for hearing and seeing in a sensitive condition.

THE BRONTËS IN IRELAND

However that may have been, his sober and earnest account of the monstrous spectre, confirming as it did the wildest stories of the Brontës, created a profound impression.

Captain Mayne Reid was then a student in Mr. McKee's school. Ghost stories were entirely in young Reid's line, and he took great delight in finding out and piecing together the different accounts of those who had been frightened by the supernatural visitors of the haunted Glen. He sometimes mingled his own yarn with the Brontë tales, and he finally ended by producing a Texan tale, called after the Brontës' crack ghost—*The Headless Horseman.*

Captain Mayne Reid's stories were received with wild excitement in the old school from which he had gone forth. *The White Chief, The War Trail, The Scalp Hunters,* were looked upon as the most wonderful tales that had ever been told ; but when *The Headless Horseman* appeared on a mustang without a scrap of mystery or element of the supernatural, all felt that the real headless horseman had been degraded to base ends, and that Captain Mayne Reid had become a fumbler in his art. I do not think his old chums ever delighted in anything he wrote afterwards.

The palmy days of the Glen ghosts had passed before my day. Familiarity with the scenes and stories had to some extent bred contempt. Perhaps,

THE BRONTËS AND THE GHOSTS 217

too, I belonged to a less imaginative and more realistic set ; but I well remember the awful feeling of dread that used to settle down on me in silence and at night.

In Mayne Reid's school days ghost-hunting was a dissipation as much in vogue as slumming is now in London. Reid, I have heard, was brave enough by day in the ghostly regions ; but, like the rest of his companions, he had no desire to approach the haunted Glen at night.

The ghosts of the Brontë Glen have, however, fallen on commonplace times. The younger generation now living in the same romantic region have perhaps never even heard of them ; or if they have, they push the report aside as " Brontë rubbish." If one of the young farmers who now cultivate the same fields should happen to meet a ghost horse in the Glen, he would run it into his stable for the night without a superstitious thought, and clap it to the plough on the morrow. No gallivanting ghosts would now be tolerated.

Fifty or sixty years ago or earlier the numerous unearthly apparitions, or rather the accounts of them, used to darken young lives, and render the silent and solitary hours hideous with dread apprehensions; and I can say for myself that the keenest mental distress I have ever endured arose from the dread of hobgoblins and other such monsters of the imagination and the darkness. I think by

THE BRONTËS IN IRELAND

the time I was three or four years of age, certainly at the age of five, I had become acquainted with the whole hierarchy of ghosts and goblins; but of all the dreadful creatures of the imagination brought under my notice, the most real, and hence the most awful, were those of the Brontë Glen.

CHAPTER XXIII

PATRICK BRONTË'S CHILDHOOD AND EARLY SURROUNDINGS

PATRICK BRONTË first saw the light in the little Emdale cottage in the parish of Drumgooland on the 17th of March, 1777. That day was Ireland's great national holiday, and the child was named Patrick as a tribute to the national sentiment, and a compliment to his uncle Patrick, known as "Red Paddy." There was a touch of Ulster shrewdness in starting the child in life with a name so comprehensive, that it did honour at the same time to Ireland's patron saint and to his own richest relative.

The Bedawi child, when born in the desert tent, stares at the sun and wonders. The first object that must have attracted the attention of baby Patrick was the red eye of the corn-kiln in the kitchen. The little fellow used to roll about, not much encumbered with garments, on the heap of dry seeds from which his father *beeked* the kiln.

From the earliest moment of intelligence the

THE BRONTËS IN IRELAND

child had an opportunity of becoming acquainted with his father's tales, and even before he could take in the meaning of the narrative he used to listen with the rest, for a child will listen to a good story-teller when he does not apprehend the drift of the story, and as a rule young children get too little credit for understanding what their elders say.

By the time he was six or seven years of age he must have known all his father's stories, which, in romantic interest and as a mental stimulant, were equal to a considerable library. Hugh Brontë was a man of two books. He was a constant reader of the Bible and of Bunyan's *Pilgrim's Progress*, and by the time Patrick was eight he would know all the stories in both books in outline.

Patrick was not long the only child in the cottage. Every second year a brother or a sister succeeded, until the family numbered ten.

There was no luxurious living in Hugh Brontë's cottage, and Patrick never regretted the want of it, for he sought to conduct his own household on lines of simple frugality. Possibly he erred in trying to bring up his delicate little girls in the Spartan style in which he himself had been reared ; but there is reason to believe that in this matter, as in many others, Mrs. Gaskell exaggerated the facts, to add to the sombre character of the picture which she chose to produce.

PATRICK BRONTË'S CHILDHOOD 221

The style of living in the cottage was very simple. Patrick's breakfast, about nine o'clock, consisted of porridge and milk, furnished in a wooden noggin and eaten with a wooden spoon For dinner, about twelve o'clock, a quantity of potatoes boiled in their skins was emptied on a table within a wooden hoop which kept them from rolling off. The poorest peasant in Ireland knows how to boil potatoes, so that when turned out on the table they appear "laughing out of their skins." Any moisture that may have remained in the vessel with the potatoes either dripped from the table on to the earthen floor or evaporated.

The children sat round the table, peeled the potatoes with their fingers, and ate them with pepper and salt, and sometimes with a supply of buttermilk. "Sweet milk" from the cow then cost a halfpenny per quart, and buttermilk six quarts a penny. As, however, the Brontës lived near their uncle Paddy, they would probably be well supplied with milk, and after a time they had a cow of their own. "Piece-time," eagerly awaited, arrived about four o'clock in the afternoon, and each child received a piece of home-made bread and a small noggin of buttermilk.

There were at that time three kinds of home-made bread : oat-bread, much thicker and coarser than the same article at the present day; then there was *fadge*, made of the potatoes remaining

THE BRONTËS IN IRELAND

over from dinner and oatmeal mashed up well together, and rolled out in the form of thick cakes ; then there was *slim*, made of potatoes broken up very fine and mixed with flour and butter. The raised soda *bap*, or scone, came later. All these kinds of bread were baked on a griddle, or girdle, which was hung over an open fire. The baking process was called "harning," and the mashing up of the potatoes with meal and flour into cakes was called "baking."

Of these three kinds of bread, the mainstay of the Brontë family was the *fadge*. It was rough and plenteous, and the sturdy little people throve well upon it, and they were not fastidious.

It was often followed by *heartburn* or *waterbrash*, which the sufferers had not learnt to call by the fine Greek name "dyspepsia."

Supper, which was served by six or seven o'clock, consisted in Patrick Brontë's childhood of potatoes, and was a stereotyped repetition of the dinner, except that the quantity was less, and the meal was not treated in so serious a fashion.

About the same time, "boiled milk," as it was called, began to alternate with potatoes for supper. It consisted of thin porridge made with milk instead of water. The boiled milk was greatly appreciated, but it was a step on the road to luxury.

A new kind of porridge known as *sowans* was

PATRICK BRONTË'S CHILDHOOD   223

also discovered ; it was sometimes called *flummery*. Sowans was produced by placing the seeds sifted from the meal in an earthenware crock, and pouring hot water on them till they were thoroughly saturated. That was called the steeping process. After twelve hours the seeds were wrung out of the water, and the fluid which remained, and which had become almost like milk, was strained into a pot, which was placed over a fire and stirred incessantly with a potstick till it thickened. Sowans was only sufficiently cooked when on lifting the potstick it ran down from it, attenuated like a thread, " fine enough to thread a needle."

A supper of sowans was considered a great delicacy, and was supposed to be good for delicate people ; but the children always preferred the boiled milk porridge.

On certain important days, such as Christmas Day and Easter Sunday, meat would find a place in the domestic economy. Uncle Paddy killed an aged cow yearly, and the beef, when salted, was hung up to the black rafters in the kitchen. Sometimes also a pig was killed, and salted for home use, and portions of such dainties found their way to the Brontë children. Eggs, too, were introduced at dinner instead of milk, and, beaten up with mashed potatoes in noggins, were eaten raw.

The greatest of all dainties, however, accessible at that period to people like the Brontës was

THE BRONTËS IN IRELAND

peppermint-tea. Peppermint and horehound were cultivated, cut, dried, and hung up to the rafters in little bunches, and a few stalks, infused with abundant milk and sugar, provided the family tea. But the new beverage was much condemned as a luxury, and it marred a girl's matrimonial prospects to have it said of her that she was a " tea-drinker."

By-and-by peppermint-tea came to be used at piece-time in the harvest field, and harvesters used to stipulate to have it supplied to them, as servants now bargain for beer. But even then, and for long after, farmers and workmen continued to regard " tea-drinking girls" as likely to prove extravagant wives.

Young Patrick would be occupied in gathering peppermint in the Glen and cultivating it in the garden. It would be his share of the work to cut it and care for it. He would go to the grocer-house for sugar, then very dear. He would fetch milk from Uncle Paddy's, and he would gather the ducks' eggs, which were generally to be found in the furze bushes. He would have a hand in " harning" the bread and stirring the sowans, and he would bear a large share in tending the other children. He would fetch water in a bucket from the well, and sweep the floor ; and in the constant round of home errands his young life must have been brimful of domestic duties.

By the time Patrick had reached the age of nine

he had to take his share in the important agricultural operation of gathering potatoes. The work for children is very hard, and requires a quick eye, prompt decision, and great nimbleness and endurance. Potato-gathering is of two kinds : gathering " to the spade," or " pitched out." In gathering to the spade, one gatherer accompanies each digger. When the digger drives his spade into the ground behind the potato plant, the gatherer darts forward, seizes the tops of the potato, then springs back as the plant is dug up, shakes the tubers from the stalks, throws the tops into a heap on the ridge and the potatoes into a basket, and then springs forward again, seizes the tops of the next potato about to be dug, and goes through the same process.

It is a pretty sight to see a healthy, active boy skipping over the ground gathering potatoes ; but when the work continues throughout a long day it is a severe task. A boy can gather the pitched-out potatoes dug by two men ; but he does not attend closely on the spades.

In potato-gathering the boys are barefooted. In the summer-time the work is hard and detested by boys ; but potatoes have generally to be gathered in the dreary months of September and October, often in the rain and sleet ; and it is a piteous sight to see the poor little barefooted children shivering, with feet and hands blue with cold, and sometimes bleeding, as they follow the diggers from grey dawn

226 *THE BRONTËS IN IRELAND*

to set of sun. Patrick took his part in potato-gathering till he had reached the age of fourteen.

Up to that age it is not likely that he ever had a pair of shoes on his feet. It is just possible that kind Uncle Paddy may have provided his namesake with a pair; but if so they would not be intended for common use; and if he went on an errand, say to Rathfriland, he would carry the shoes in his hand till he reached the town, and take them off his feet again on leaving for home. Shoes were worn in those days by such boys as Brontë chiefly as ornaments. Had Patrick gone to church, he would most probably have carried his shoes in his hands to the church door, and have put them on before entering; unlike the Arabs, who always remove their shoes before going into a place of worship.

During those years young Brontë was always clad in home-spun. Most of his garments were knitted by his mother, and were very enduring and excellent in every way. They were warm, fitted neatly, and set off his lithe figure to perfection.

To the eyes of boys in tailor-made habiliments he looked a guy, and his odd appearance was supposed to have some connection with his mongrel origin. In his tights he looked taller and slenderer than he really was; and as he became the subject of constant ridicule and jeering, he was often engaged in the operation of chastising boys who looked twice as robust as himself.

PATRICK BRONTË'S CHILDHOOD 227

His youth was harassed with perpetual strife. The Protestant lads never lost an opportunity of calling him "Mongrel Pat," or "Pat the Papish," and the odium of his mother's early religion clung to him until he got clear of Ireland. Indeed, the slur which was cast upon him on account of his mother's religion was the determining cause which led finally to his decision to leave his native country.

At the age of fourteen it was thought desirable to put him to some trade. He had spent much of his time about the Emdale blacksmith's shop. He used to blow the bellows, and he became very expert in welding scrap-iron. He also got so far as to be able to make horseshoes and nails from Swedish iron ; but he could not become a black-smith without being bound as an apprentice for five years, and his father was too much of a radical to submit to such an absurd arrangement.

The trade of weaver also demanded an apprenticeship, but only of two years' duration, and Robert Donald, a friend of the Brontës, consented to take Patrick as a learner without the usual formalities. He made good progress in acquiring skill in his art, and before long he was able to supply the Brontë home with all the blankets and druggets and tweeds that were needed.

About that period flax began to be extensively cultivated and manufactured in Ulster, and Patrick learned to weave linen, and used to carry his webs

THE BRONTËS IN IRELAND

when finished to Banbridge, where he found a ready sale. Those were war times. Flax cost a pound per stone then, which would be worth five or six shillings now. Linen became correspondingly dear, and young Brontë became prosperous. But his prosperity led to a change of occupation.*

The weaver boy used to visit bookstalls in Banbridge and Newry, and on one occasion he took his web to Belfast, and returned laden with books. His father's tales created in the lad a hunger for literature, a passion easily kindled in a Celtic boy, and he learned to weave and read at the same time, with his book propped up before him.

---

* Mr. Frazer, now over ninety-two years of age, assures the Rev. J. B. Lusk that the Brontës were for a time Catholics. He gives the following account of Patrick's conversion : " He was weaving in the house of Robert Donald, a Presbyterian, and a very pious man. Donald conducted family worship every morning and night. Patrick overheard him reading and praying. He became interested, asked questions, and finally ended by becoming a Protestant." I cannot reconcile this with other facts.

Mr. Frazer is the oldest living witness as to the name Brontë, which he never saw spelled differently from the ordinary way. There is also a lease of a farm given by Joseph Frazer to Hugh Brontë, signed by Hugh Brontë and James Brontë in the usual orthography. He is, I believe, the only survivor of the multitude who witnessed the Brontë battle eighty-two years ago.

CHAPTER XXIV

PATRICK BRONTË'S SCHOOLS AND SCHOOL-MASTERS—LEARNING AND WEAVING

PATRICK BRONTË at the age of fifteen or sixteen appeared to be permanently fixed in his profession as a weaver. The foundations of the Ulster linen trade were then being laid. Flax seed from Riga and Amsterdam had begun to be imported into Newry and Belfast, and the farmers were gradually learning to grow and manufacture flax for the markets. The meadows on the banks of the river Bann were being turned into bleach-greens, and the holmes of Down began to gleam white with webs spread out to bleach.

Patrick Brontë was a good weaver. He flew the shuttle and clecked the sleys with deftness and skill, and he was able to earn good wages at his trade. A small matter, however, turned the whole current of his career, just as circumstances with small beginnings had led his father from the lime-kilns of Louth to the corn-kiln of County Down.

He had become so expert a weaver that he

THE BRONTËS IN IRELAND

was able to attend to both loom and book at the same time. And the more he read his appetite for book lore increased the more. His earnings enabled him by the acquisition of books to indulge his growing thirst for knowledge. He had secured a small copy of Milton's *Paradise Lost*. He had never come under the spell of such a book before, and he read and re-read it incessantly. The type was very minute, and as he was absorbed in the subject of the epic he failed in his attention to the work he had in hand.

He had got a commission from a Banbridge linen merchant to weave him a number of webs of unusual fineness. The merchant had provided him with a fine reed, and supplied him with the yarn ; and young Brontë, as a skilled weaver, seemed to be on the road to success, as the pay for very fine work was much above that paid for ordinary weaving. He was, however, a few days beyond contract time in delivering his second web, and when it was handed in it was found to be unsatisfactory.

In those days linen was classified and registered according to its texture, its quality being regulated by the number of threads to the inch. When the merchant placed his magnifying-glass on Patrick's web, he found that the warp had not been regularly and evenly driven home, and he fined him heavily for imperfect work.

PATRICK BRONTË'S SCHOOLS

The young weaver returned home disgraced and crestfallen. He could not and would not give up his reading ; but he felt that he could not carry on his trade with a divided mind. He resolved therefore that he would give a part of each day to reading and a part to weaving, and endeavour to concentrate his attention on each task while engaged upon it.

He was not very successful in adjusting the claims of his intellectual and mechanical occupations, for Milton's good and bad angels kept running over the thread stretched out before him, and he was always waking up to find that he had been plying the shuttle in a reverie, and that serious defects had escaped his notice, and were already rolled on the cloth beam.

While he was in this condition of double-mindedness, he was lying one summer day prone on the grass in Emdale fort, reading the *Paradise Lost.* The Rev. Andrew Harshaw, who happened to pass that way, drew near and stood over the reader, and remained listening to him for a considerable time. Patrick was reciting aloud bits of Milton in a kind of absent-minded frenzy, and making comments as he read with great energy. Suddenly looking up, he became conscious that a man was standing over him. He sprang to his feet blushing, and apparently overwhelmed with shame. Harshaw spoke kindly to the youth, and entering

THE BRONTËS IN IRELAND

into intelligent conversation with him about the passage he had read, led him on to tell him of the manner in which he was neglecting his work, and of his inability to keep his mind fixed on his task.

Harshaw and young Brontë, deeply engaged in serious conversation, walked arm in arm round the Emdale fort, the remains of which are still visible. As Brontë listened to his new friend he felt as if his whole life had become transformed. Harshaw opened up a vista of possibilities to the depressed youth, who in his kindling enthusiasm saw everything in the light of his own glowing imagination. In his eyes the drab and dull earth had become instinct with life and colour, and seemed bathed in a divine light never seen before. The lingering snow that streaked the Mourne Mountains appeared to glow with a roseate hue, and even the sombre summit of the Knock Hill was lighted up with golden gorse.

Never before to Brontë's ears had the thrush in the Glen sung so sweetly, or the lark flooded the skies with such rapturous music. Even the humming of the bees among the clover was sweetly melodious, and the monotopous echoes of the cuckoo from the leafy sycamore sounded as notes of courage and hope.

Who was the Rev. Andrew Harshaw? He was related in a remote way to the Harshaws of Loughorne, who had been so kind to old Hugh, Patrick's

PATRICK BRONTË'S SCHOOLS

father. They certainly had a family likeness, and the Brontës, father and son, owed an incalculable debt of gratitude to the Harshaws, to whom English literature also is under an abiding obligation.

The Rev. Andrew Harshaw was what was commonly called a "stickit minister." He had been educated and trained for the ministry of the Presbyterian Church ; but as the ministers of that Church were called by the free suffrages of the people to whom they were to minister, and as he lacked pulpit power, he failed to gain a pastorate.

He was said to have been the first Irish Presbyterian minister who wrote out and read his sermons, and no congregation would in those days have dreamt of calling a man who took a written sermon with him to the pulpit. "If he cannot remember what he is going to tell us," said an old lady, "when he has all the week to think about it, how could he expect us to remember it on hearing it only once drawled out from his copy-book?"

Mr. Harshaw was, however, a first-rate scholar and a godly man. He had completed an under graduate course of four years with distinction, and he had afterwards passed some six years in theological studies, in addition to a long preparatory school training. In fact, his school and college career had been singularly brilliant ; but the work of absorbing knowledge is very different from that of giving it out in effective and eloquent words, and so the performance of his manhood fell far short of the promise of his youth.

There are few sadder sights than that of the brilliant student of the university trying to live up to the standard of his early achievements and reputation, but passed in the race by men on whom he had looked down at college, and forgotten in a utilitarian age, which recks little of brilliant scholastic traditions, and tests everything by its effectiveness. Harshaw, besides being an excellent classical and mathematical scholar, was deeply read in English literature. He had outlived his ambitions, and settled down patiently to teach a little school in Ballynafern. The school is there to this day, but I believe the schoolhouse has been rebuilt and enlarged. It stands on a high hill, not far from where the Brontës lived, and commands a splendid view of the surrounding country.

I believe Harshaw had a farm close to the school, and it is not unlikely that he preferred the learned leisure of attending to his school and farm, to the incessant preparation of sermons and the stated visitation of families involved in a country pastorate. I have always understood that he was an indolent dreamer, although a contemplative enthusiast.

Patrick Brontë was just the kind of youth to draw out the full sympathy of this unappreciated scholar. He was helpless and unhappy in his sordid

PATRICK BRONTË'S SCHOOLS 235

surroundings. He was hungering for knowledge. His aspirations were high, but he was chained by the exigencies of life to the monotonous existence of a common weaver. He was in revolt against the task by which he earned his daily bread because it allowed no time to feed his mind. From Harshaw he learned how he might exchange the earthen vessel of the weaver for the golden bowl of the scholar. Before Harshaw and Brontë parted on that summer day plans were laid for the youth's future career. Harshaw agreed to lend him books and to teach him. Brontë was to cultivate his loom, not as a rival to learning, but as its auxiliary and handmaid. He returned to his weaving with something of the spirit in which Jacob laboured to win the beauteous Rachel ; and though, like Jacob, he often found himself clasping the blear-eyed Leah, he worked on in the teeth of disappointment, and never bated heart or hope until he had secured the highest objects of his ambition.

Artificial lights within reach of the Brontës were in those days very poor. Rushlights were simply the pith of peeled rushes dipped in melted tallow. They gave a very dim light, and burnt quickly. The more common lights were rosin-sluts. These were also manufactured at home. A few pounds of rosin were melted in a deep pan called a *kam*, and long strings held at the two ends were dipped in the hot melted rosin. The wick was turned round in the rosin until it had taken on a sufficient quantity, and then with the attached fluid was rolled by the palms of the hands on a table until it became round like a candle. The rosin-sluts gave better light than the rushlights, but they sputtered a good deal, required constant snuffing, and were otherwise objectionable as lights to weave by.

Besides these there were splits made from bog fir ; but they had to be held in the hand while burning, and rubbed against each other to remove the black burnt part. Most of the reading in farmhouses in those days was done by the firelight, assisted by splits ; but a weaver could not carry on his work dependent on such precarious light.

As Brontë could not weave fine linen by any of those lights, his work at the loom was limited to the hours of daylight. He wove incessantly, and with his whole heart in his work, from grey dawn to dusky eve. The remainder of his time he had at his disposal for rest and study. He rose early and sat up late, and studied assiduously by the light of splits.

During his first years of study young Brontë never allowed himself more than five hours' sleep at night, and in the dark hours he used to sit in his uncle Paddy's chimney corner reading Ovid and Virgil and Homer and Herodotus, and working out the problems of Euclid on the hearthstone with the blackened end of his half-burnt splits.

A couple of hours before dawn he went to Harshaw, who received him in his bedroom, and taught him by the light of a rosin-slut free of all charge. Harshaw often taught his pupil leaning on his elbow in bed ; but he always insisted that he should be at his loom in time to begin his work as soon as daylight permitted.

Patrick Brontë worked like a man determined to conquer all his disadvantages. Perhaps those were his happiest days. While he studied he concentrated all the powers of his intellect on his lessons, and he put into the weaving all the skill of which he was capable.

Harshaw praised his ability, and predicted a brilliant career for the student, and the merchant had no further cause to complain of slovenly weaving.

CHAPTER XXV

LEARNING AND TEACHING

PATRICK BRONTË had laboured heroically at his two tasks for about a year, when his Banbridge employer suddenly died, and he was thrown out of work. None of the Banbridge merchants wanted linen of such fine texture, and Brontë did not care to fall back on coarse and ill-paid work. He had saved money, and was able for a time to give all his hours to study. Harshaw saw that he had reached a period when he might safely give up his loom altogether, and live for the future by education.

At that time a teacher was wanted for the school in connection with Glascar Hill Presbyterian Church. Harshaw applied for the school for his pupil Brontë; but the managers did not consider a youth whose mother was a Roman Catholic a suitable person to teach Presbyterian children. Besides this there was some danger that the Orange party would not send their children to be taught by a Brontë. Another candidate was appointed to the post, but something prevented him from accepting the situation, and in the hour of disappointment the minister of the congregation, the Rev. Alexander Moore, appointed Brontë teacher on his own responsibility.

GLASCAR SCHOOL, WHERE PATRICK BRONTË FIRST TAUGHT.

The Brontës, who lived less than a mile from the Glascar school, were known as people who went regularly to no place of worship on Sundays. Occasionally some of them dropped into Glascar Meeting House at the time of public worship; but such casual attendance did little to remove the

THE BRONTËS IN IRELAND

stigma of living like the heathen. They seldom repeated their visits, for they were proud people, and did not like to be stared at as reprobates.

From the time of his appointment young Brontë attended regularly at the Presbyterian service, and assisted in conducting the music. His brothers and sisters also became regular worshippers at Glascar, and he himself became soon a favourite both in the school and in the Church, except with a few extreme Orangemen, who never missed an opportunity of reminding him of his mother's religion.

It is still remembered that "Master Brontë" studied the characters of his pupils, and dealt with each one according to his abilities. In this matter he differed widely from the ordinary school teacher, who makes no difference between clever boys and dull boys, and labours like a drill sergeant to make all march by the same line and rule. There is no profession in the world in which one sees learning and common sense so absolutely divorced as in that of the school teacher.

The little boy with the bright eye and massive head of the scholar is at the top of the class with scarcely an effort, while the leaden-eyed, sloping-headed scion of a race of dunces is toiling with his featherweight of brains at the bottom of the class. The boy with ten talents is praised and petted, and rewarded for doing the work that the boy with one

LEARNING AND TEACHING

talent is expected to do ; and the boy with one talent is bullied and punished for not doing the same lesson as the boy with ten talents.

Those were the good old whipping days, only the taws fell on the wrong palms. The teachers should have been whipped for beating dull boys because they could not learn lessons that they had neither brains nor heart to learn.

Patrick Brontë began on a different plan. He found out what each pupil could do and liked to do, and he endeavoured to educate them on the lines of their own gifts and qualifications. By education he sought to draw out and develop the faculties with which they were endowed. Teaching on these lines, he had no occasion to exercise physical force. He brought common sense or "gumption" to his work, and he required no taws.

The pupils of Glascar school were largely the children of farmers and workpeople. When the master came upon a child preternaturally dull, he did not harass him as a blockhead, or make his life miserable as a dunce. He never let the school, or even the boy himself, suspect that he was dull ; but he put him to easy lessons that were necessary to qualify him for the narrow sphere in which his life would in all probability be cast, and the pupil worked at these with hearty goodwill and intelligence.

But when he found a clever student he let him

have full swing in the higher branches, and several little country boys who began their studies under Brontë succeeded in forcing their ways to the universities, and some of them became professional men of eminence.

To all the pupils who came under his influence he communicated a taste for learning in their own spheres, which they never forgot ; and some of them who were unable to reach the university themselves were careful to let their children have the advantages that they had missed.

During the short time he was teacher at Glascar, Master Brontë put new life into the school. He became the friend of all his pupils, and visited their parents to advise as to their careers. The dull pupils he sent home to help their parents ; but he established a night-school in which they might practise what they had learnt, and learn more if they were so inclined.

At the night-school amusement was added to lessons, and there was no difficulty in drawing pupils. Before the classes broke up, the young people were put through a series of gymnastics, and a number of Church tunes were sung, each pupil repeating the words he wished to be sung, and raising his own tune. Brontë thus sought to quicken intelligence in the dull pupils, for whom the night-school was principally intended.

But when Brontë found really bright pupils he

LEARNING AND TEACHING

was loth to part with them, and so earnestly did he plead with their parents that many of them permitted their children to remain at school longer than they otherwise would have done, that they might enjoy the training of their enthusiastic young teacher.

On this subject the Rev. W. J. McCracken of Ballyeaston writes me as follows :—

" My mother was a pupil of Patrick Brontë when he taught the school at Glascar Hill. I heard her say so many a time. She was also a favourite scholar with him ; for when she was withdrawn from school to help in household work, she being the eldest of a large family, Patrick Brontë came to her father's house, and besought them to send her back and keep at home another sister, whom he considered a dull girl. Patrick must have been teaching this school about the beginning of the century, as my mother was six years old at the time of the rebellion."

Many such traditions still linger in the Glascar district. Master Brontë did not limit his pupils to the ordinary school-books. The despotic system of competitive examinations on the Chinese model had not then been established in country schools, and children were not treated simply as smooth bores, and charged to the muzzles with text-books, to be belched forth on testing days, leaving nothing behind but wasted residuum. They could touch subjects of interest that did not *tell* in examinations, and so the young teacher introduced them to Milton's *Paradise Lost*, and other masterpieces of English literature.

They took the teacher's book home at night in turn, copied out their pieces, and then recited them at the close of school hours, or at the night-school. The young people's minds were thus stored with noble forms of speech and glowing thoughts, and the wave of intelligence and literary taste set in motion at Glascar in the closing years of last century cannot be said to have quite died away.

Mr. Harshaw continued to teach and advise young Brontë, although the Glascar school had become a formidable rival to that of Ballynafern. He saw that his pupil had capacity for a higher sphere than that of school teacher at Glascar, where each pupil paid one penny per week for education, and brought one *turf* every Monday morning towards the heating of the school.

Education opened three doors to young men like Patrick Brontë in those days. He might have continued a teacher, and by ability, humility, and patronage, have risen in time to command a salary of £30 or £40 per annum; or he might with great perseverance, spending years as a chemist's assistant, have worked through a medical curriculum and obtained an easy M.D. at Glasgow University; or he might, regardless of the limitations of human

LEARNING AND TEACHING 245

life, have entered on a course of eight years'
study, with a view to becoming a minister of the
Presbyterian Church.

Mr. Harshaw, as a Presbyterian minister, might
have been expected to guide the youth to the gate
from which he himself had emerged, trailing clouds
of glory; but he was an honest man, and he did
not. He knew that Brontë was a youth of ability,
and of enthusiastic temperament; but he knew that
the Presbyterian Church demanded graces as well
as gifts in her ministers, and had testing questions on the subject, and he did not believe that
Brontë's spiritual nature had ever been kindled or
quickened. He therefore advised him to choose
as a profession the Episcopal ministry.

Those were the days of moderatism and frigid
formalism in the Irish Episcopal Church. The
clergy had to maintain the status and perform
the duties of country gentlemen. They had little
sympathy with the people, and when they read
their little homilies to their flocks the hungry
sheep looked up and were not fed.

There were in the ranks of the Irish clergy, even
in those days of spiritual death, noble Christian
ministers, who did not neglect the poor to pay
court to the rich; but such men were a small
minority. The duties of the holy office were not
supposed to stand in the way of a man who wished
to devote himself to business pursuits or to amuse-

ments, or even to the common dissipations of the rich, so long as they did not lead to open scandal.

With many brilliant exceptions, the Episcopal ministry was largely recruited, in the north of Ireland, from men who had found the way into the Presbyterian ministry too long, and the gate too narrow. The Episcopal Church was an open haven for those who had failed in their examinations, either at the hands of the Presbytery or of the University. And many a young man in a hurry had reason to thank the strict old Presbyterian minister who *stuck* him in his examination for not knowing something about Moses and Peter.

The *pluckt* youth disappeared, but after an absence of about three years reappeared in the neighbouring parish in all the latest feathers of his profession, and remained a country gentleman and magistrate, the finest social figure in the district, except the land agent. A change for the better has taken place, and the minister of the Disestablished Episcopalian Church in Ireland would now compare favourably in gifts, graces, scholarship, and effectiveness with the ministers of any Church in the kingdom.

Harshaw, during his long undergraduate course, had had to fight his upward way unaided. He had spent several years as a tutor in England, and he strongly advised his brilliant pupil to seek orders in the Church of England. A college course of

LEARNING AND TEACHING 247

three or four years, instead of eight, would suffice.

He assured him that he would find the English a fair-minded people, who would value him for his work ; and that as a clergyman he would have plenty of honest work to do in teaching and preaching and visiting, as well as plenty of honest leisure for self-improvement and the authorship to which he looked forward. Above all, he would escape for ever from the cry of "Mongrel" and "Papish Pat" that every Protestant urchin shouted after him on account of his mother's maiden religion.

Perhaps, indeed, the circumstance that more than any other determined Brontë to seek an asylum in England was the fact that his beautiful and loving mother had, when a girl, belonged to the Roman Catholic Church, and the odium attaching to the circumstance could never, among a bigoted people, be lived down, since the fact could not be altered.

The mixed character of Patrick Brontë's origin was a fact kept well before his mind every day of his life in Ireland by the youths with whom he mingled. At first the insult led to battles, but his assailants were numerous, and brave in proportion to the superiority of their numbers, and a man with "black papish blood" in him was a common enemy.

Brontë seldom emerged from the strife victorious,

248 *THE BRONTËS IN IRELAND*

and so he schooled himself to bear the stinging gibes and bigoted insolence in sullen silence; and sometimes, as in the Glascar school, he made friends even of his enemies.

Brontë's speculations as to his future career gave wings to his imagination and spurred him in his studies, and after three years' close application he had mastered all the classical and mathematical books in Harshaw's library. He continued to teach the school with great zeal, and to read and re-read all the ancient and modern literature he could lay his hands on.

About this period he made the acquaintance of the Rev. David Barber, Presbyterian minister of Rathfriland, and from him he was able to borrow such books as Spenser's *Faërie Queene*, the *Spectator*, Hume's *History of England*, and, above all, Shakespeare's works. To a youth like Brontë these volumes brought great joy.

At Glascar school it was not "all work and no play." The master led his pupils, two and two, on Saturdays to visit the different places of interest in the neighbourhood, and on those expeditions he tried to make them see the beauty of the landscape. He would stop them on the way, and draw their attention to the lights and shadows chasing each other over the fields, to the curves of hills and mountains, to the different ways in which birds flew, and to the hidden beauties of the common

LEARNING AND TEACHING

flowers that bloomed by the waysides. Some of the pupils said he was mad, but others received sight to discern the unnoticed beauties of the things that lay around them.

During the summer holidays he organised more ambitious expeditions. On several occasions he led the older boys and some of their elder brothers to explore the Mourne Mountains. On one of those trips the party got separated on Slieve Donnard, and a thick mist having overspread the mountain the explorers lost their way ; and as they did not return home at the appointed time, much alarm was caused to their families.

It was several days before they all reached home, footsore and exhausted, but rich with romantic stories of hairbreadth escapes and thrilling adventures, which served as travellers' tales for the remainder of their lives.

Skating expeditions to Loughorne and Loughbrickland gave scope for daring feats and startling adventures. On one occasion the water had been drawn off from the lough, and when the party were in the middle of it, and far from land, the ice broke with a roar like thunder ; but Brontë kept cool, and steered his whole party safe to the shore.

While teaching in Glascar Brontë blossomed into poetry. Most of the pieces published in 1811 among his *Cottage Poems* were written in Glascar.

THE BRONTËS IN IRELAND

One of them, which referred to the adventure on the Mourne Mountains, was learnt and recited in the school, and gained for the author a great name as a poet. Some of the lines, which are probably still remembered in the neighbourhood, ran as follows :—

> "Escaped from the pitiless storm,
>   I entered the humble retreat ;
> Compact was the building and warm,
>   In furniture simple and neat.
> And now, gentle reader, approve
>   The ardour that glowed in each breast,
> As kindly our cottagers strove
>   To cherish and welcome their guest."

"The Irish Cabin," which also appeared in *Cottage Poems*, was very popular, and much recited by the pupils and their friends ; and there were other poems, such as "The Cottage Maid" and "The Happy Cottager," which were copied out by the scholars from Brontë's manuscript and learned by heart.

In those days the young master was a most voluminous poet, and I have little doubt that most of the pieces which were published in 1811 took form in Glascar about 1797, and were touched up in after-years in England for publication.

The *Cottage Poems* have recently been subjected to severe criticism ; but it should be remembered that they were really the work of a weaver lad, who was just then awakening to the pleasures of

LEARNING AND TEACHING 251

literature, and that they were written for the children of farmers and labourers in a poor country school.

Besides, the poems published are only such as a prudent clergyman should have given to the world. They were pure in sentiment, kindly in tone, flowing in rhyme, and contained nothing extreme that could have startled a patron. But Brontë left out other poems in which his distinctive genius had had full scope. Such pieces as "The Devil in the Glen," "The Emigrant's Lament," and "Kitty's Revenge" were charged with Brontë passion, and were not lacking in poetic fire.

He had, however, eaten the bread of a sizar at Cambridge; he had taken his full share of the duties and recreations that make up University life; he had got his foot on the ladder of promotion, and his eyes on the dispensers of livings; and so he published in 1811 his weak moral musings, and kept back the fierce and fiery shrieks of his newly awakened genius.

Moreover, Brontë had come to know the English people, and he had found them fair and just, and his temper had lost the hot fire and keen edge which oppressing circumstances had given it. Like many another Irish Samson, the locks of his strength were shorn in the lap of the English Delilah; or rather, the old neglected truth had another illustration in the case of Brontë—namely, that kindness and courtesy breed love and gentleness.

THE BRONTËS IN IRELAND

I have hesitated as to whether I should give a characteristic specimen of Patrick Brontë's ferocious poetry, and I here with some reluctance insert his " Vision of Hell," written in Glascar. I feel that I must at least give one sample, if the readers of this book are to have full material for coming to a correct judgment as to the Brontë genius, and the antecedent influences that led to the production of the Brontë novels, especially of *Wuthering Heights*.

" VISION OF HELL.

" At midnight, alone, in the lonely dell,
Through a rent I beheld the court of hell ;
I stood struck dumb by the horrid spell
Of the tide of wailing that rose and fell.

" The devil sat squat on a fine-winged throne ;
Before him in ranks lay his victims prone ;
In anguish they praised him with sullen groan,
Like an ocean that never ceased to moan.

" At a signal they sprang from their burning bed,
And through sulphurous flames, by devils led,
In mazy dances they onward sped,
As they followed the devils who danced ahead.

" ' Enough ! ' yelled the fiend from the fire-winged throne,
' Of posture-praise from my subjects prone,
Of torture, shrieks, and of sullen moan,
Of mazy dances and stifled groan.

" ' Each to his post in my burnished state.
Ye clergy, who fed the fires of hate,
Neglected the poor, and cringed to the great,
Ye shall roast in honour within my grate.

LEARNING AND TEACHING

"'I dread no foe but the Christ of God;
Through you, His clergy, I feared His rod;
But you took His pay and obeyed my nod,
And you drove the poor from their native sod.

"'Ye landlords can only have second place,
In devilish deeds ye were first in the race;
But no treason to Christ mixed with your disgrace,
Ye were mine from the first, and in every place.

"'Attorneys and agents, I love you well,
But you throng with your numbers the courts of hell;
Bastard-bearers and bailiffs need place as well,
For their hellish deeds no tongue can tell.

"The clergy aloft on a burning floor
Sat slaking their thirst with bastards' gore,
And gnawing the bones of the murdered poor,
The evicted who died on the silent moor.

"The landlords were penned in a fiery fold,
And drank from a furnace of molten gold
The rent they had wrung from their tenants of old,
Who had laboured and died in hunger and cold.

---

* This refers to the fact that taxes were levied by the clergy
and their Church officers for the transport of illegitimate
children to the foundling hospital in Dublin. The "bastard-
bearers" were vile creatures who pocketed their pay, and
dropped their burdens into bog-holes. Bog water has astrin-
gent qualities that prevent decay, and the remains of
infants were very often dug up in bogs by turf-cutters. The
vestry minutes of Drumballyroney Church show that the tax
was still levied on the people at the time that Patrick Brontë
taught there. The deportation of illegitimate children was
almost a wholesale system of murder, and Patrick Brontë in
his early years laid the blame at the door of those who levied
the tax and superintended the system. The poem, which was
much longer, was written about 1796 or 1797.

254 *THE BRONTËS IN IRELAND*

> " And the men who had paid for love by lust,
> And were false in return for confiding trust,
> In a slimy pit they were downward thrust,
> Through a scum that was foul with a fetid crust.
>
> * * * * *
>
> " And a cry arose like the thunder's roar
> As the devil stood forth on the burning floor,
> And the fiends with a shout stood up to adore,
> And the earth-rent closed and I saw no more."

Brontë's teaching in Glascar came to an abrupt termination in a very characteristic manner. There was a mature maiden in the school with hair as red as his own. She was the daughter of a substantial farmer with aristocratic tendencies, as he had more acres and more cattle than most of his neighbours. Patrick, as "the master," had always been welcome at the farmhouse. The girl and her brothers had been allowed to remain longer than usual at school at his special request, and as they were studying advanced subjects he helped them in the evening with their lessons.

One afternoon, on approaching the farmer's house, the master met his red-haired pupil among the corn-stacks and kissed her. The tender incident was observed by one of the brothers, who immediately reported the result of his observations at headquarters. War was instantly declared against the "mongrel" and "papish brat" who had dared to kiss their Helen. The allied brothers proceeded directly to chastise Brontë; but the affair became complicated by the fiery-headed Helen, *teterrima causa belli*, rushing in and espousing Brontë's cause with great spirit and vigour.

When the storm of battle had cleared away, it was discovered that teacher and pupil were des-

PRESBYTERIAN MEETING HOUSE, WHERE PATRICK BRONTË WAS PRECENTOR.

perately in love with each other, and that opposition had only fanned the flame. Helen's pockets and desk were found to be full of Patrick's amatory poetry, and both claimed the right to act as they pleased. It was understood that the first tender advances had been on the lady's part, and her lover

256 *THE BRONTËS IN IRELAND*

felt bound to remain loyal to her so long as she held out.

There were many versions of the incident, from which it would be difficult to weave one consistent narrative, nor is it a matter of much importance. One thing is certain, namely, that all the parties concerned made great fools of themselves, of whom the greatest was Patrick Brontë.

Helen's father was an important officer in the Glascar Presbyterian Church, to which a young minister, John Rogers, had just been called. The new minister was wholly unacquainted with Brontë, or with the merits of the difficulty into which he had got ; but on the representation of so influential a member of his congregation he consented to the closing of the school and the dismissal of the master. Thus Patrick Brontë, by his own folly, found himself without employment or the prospect of employment in the memorable but miserable years of 1797 and 1798.

Brontë by his imprudence had not only lost his situation and the golden-haired damsel ; but what was even more serious, he had lost his friend and teacher.

Mr. Harshaw was a sternly just man, as well as thoroughly unselfish. He upbraided Brontë for taking advantage of his position to gain an unwarrantable influence over one of his pupils without the consent or knowledge of her parents.

LEARNING AND TEACHING 257

Brontë responded with indignant anger ; in fact, he had one of his ungovernable fits, when the veins in his forehead and neck seemed ready to burst, and teacher and pupil parted in anger.

For a year, or perhaps less, Brontë worked on his Uncle Paddy's farm, and was often to be seen walking up and down the Glen with a book in his hand. During those weary days he was in the habit of meeting Helen clandestinely, as his father used to meet Alice McClory ; but Helen differed widely from Alice. She soon wearied of the derelict schoolmaster who had nothing to do but loaf about Red Paddy's farm. The brilliant student and romantic poet was a very different lover from the unhappy youth without prospects. To Helen's eyes the gold had gone off the gingerbread and the romance had ceased to thrill, and so she became the wife of an honest farmer, and the mother of a numerous fiery-headed progeny.

Brontë's first love affair having come to an end, he went back to his old and true friend Harshaw. He admitted his dishonourable conduct, apologised for his rudeness, and was taken once more into his patron's favour.

Harshaw immediately set to work to secure for his pupil another situation. The parish school of Drumballyroney was then vacant ; but it was known that only a Churchman would have any chance of being elected to the post. The appointment was

258   *THE BRONTËS IN IRELAND*

in the hands of the Rev. Thomas Tighe, the rector. Harshaw sought an interview with Mr. Tighe, and told him Patrick Brontë's history, not omitting the love scene and penitence.*   The vicar agreed to see Brontë, and the interview led to his appointment as teacher at a higher salary than he had had in Glascar.   This engagement marked another important stage in the career of Patrick Brontë.

* I purposely abstain from giving Helen's family name, as the almost forgotten story might give pain.   Her descendants are among the most respected people of the neighbourhood.

CHAPTER XXVI

PATRICK BRONTË IN AN EPISCOPALIAN SCHOOL

IT was, I believe, in the autumn of 1798 that Patrick Brontë entered on his duties at Drumballyroney. The school, which had dwindled almost to extinction under the previous teacher, revived and flourished under Brontë's care and energy.

In addition to the day-school, he had a class for private tuition, that met in the vicar's drawing-room. The class consisted of Mr. Tighe's children and the children of another local magnate. The tuition fees added to Brontë's salary as schoolmaster amounted to a sum that encouraged him to look forward once more to a University career.

I have heard of few noteworthy incidents of Brontë's life while acting as schoolmaster in Drumballyroney. He seems to have been so happy that he manufactured little or no history. If he were the hero of any very heroic or tragic exploits, they have never been recorded, and are never likely to be brought to light.

One little affair showed the metal of which he

260   *THE BRONTËS IN IRELAND*

was made.   He was leading the united Sunday and day-school out for a holiday's amusement.   The bully of the neighbourhood, a Roman Catholic, stood in the middle of a narrow path, and obliged the children to go down into a muddy ditch to get past him.

Patrick was coming behind with Mr. Tighe, but on observing the conduct of the bully, he broke away from the vicar regardless of remonstrance, and, seizing the offender by the neck and leg, flung him down the hill into the ditch and left him there.   This incident formed the groundwork of the story told by Charlotte in *Shirley*, where Helstone precipitated a similar obnoxious person into the ditch.

Mr. J. A. Erskine Stuart * tells, on the authority of Mr. Yates, an almost similar story of an event that took place on Whit-Tuesday 1810 at Earls-heaton.   I am inclined to believe that the simple and sudden collision in Drumballyroney was the genuine original of all the later versions.

The Rev. Thomas Tighe was the vicar of the united parishes of Drumballyroney and Drum-gooland for forty-three years.   He seems to have found Brontë useful in the parish school as well as in his own family, and it is exceedingly likely

---

* Mr. J. A. Erskine Stuart was the first to challenge the groundless assertion that Patrick Brontë on coming to England changed his name from Prunty to Brontë.

PATRICK BRONTË IN AN EPISCOPALIAN SCHOOL 261

that he employed the handsome and brilliant youth
in many ways in the two large parishes.

In a busy life Brontë would have less leisure for
cultivating the romantic side of his character, and
fewer opportunities for coming into collision with
the stubborn conventionalities of the district. But
though we have little positive personal information
regarding Brontë at Drumballyroney, we have
very full information regarding the parish and the
period of his sojourn in it in the volume of minutes
discovered by Mr. Lett.

CHAPTER XXVII

PATRICK BRONTË AT ST. JOHN'S, CAMBRIDGE

FROM a glance at the minutes kept by Rector Tighe, it is clear that he was a vigorous administrator at a time when vigour was needed, and that he was an educationalist when education was at a low ebb. Having found Patrick Brontë an enthusiastic and excellent teacher, he not only appreciated his services, but guided him in his efforts to obtain a University education for himself.

There is no ground for assuming, as has been done, that Brontë received pecuniary assistance from Mr. Tighe to enable him to enter the University. He had a good salary as school teacher, and to this was added a considerable sum as tuition fees. Like many other Irish students who taught during the summer months and studied at the University during the winter, he would save every penny he received beyond what was absolutely necessary for his support, and after three years in Drumballyroney he would have saved from £100 to £130, a sum amply sufficient to launch him fairly at St. John's.

Mr. Tighe doubtless gave him full information as to the exhibitions and bursaries at St. John's, and the steps to be taken by him as a candidate for honours; and such important information would be all that the youth required. He spent all his spare time in study, and on Saturdays he reviewed all the week's work with his old and true

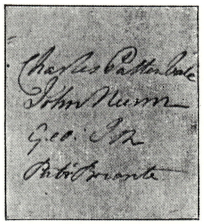

PATRICK BRONTË'S MATRICULATION SIGNATURE.

friend Harshaw. Indeed, Harshaw had been his only teacher up to the time he reached the Cambridge University.

Patrick Brontë entered St. John's College, Cambridge, on the 1st of October, 1802, and commenced residence on the fourth day of the same month. In the following February, 1803, four

THE BRONTËS IN IRELAND

months after entering the College, he obtained one of the Hare Exhibitions, which he continued to hold till March 1806.

These exhibitions had been founded by Sir Ralph Hare "for thirty of the poorest and best-disposed scholars"; but, notwithstanding the terms of the trust, the paramount consideration was scholarship, then as now, in awarding the prizes.

The Duchess of Suffolk had also left a sum to St. John's, to establish exhibitions for four poor scholars. At Christmas 1803 Brontë won one of these, and continued on the foundation as Duchess of Suffolk exhibitioner till Christmas 1807. Besides these, he won and held the Goodman Exhibition for one year from 1805.

Brontë's savings were ample to carry him over his first few months at Cambridge, and the Hare, Suffolk, and Goodman Exhibitions were quite sufficient afterwards for all his wants as a student. His friends at home, however, understood that he was living at college by coaching other students, and it was doubtless from the money earned by teaching that he forwarded the sum of £20 to his mother every year. Indeed, his first letter to his mother from Cambridge announcing his admission to St. John's contained a half-sovereign under the seal, and during her life he never failed to write regularly to her, both while he was at Cambridge and afterwards, and, whatever his circumstances

PATRICK BRONTË AT ST. JOHN'S, CAMBRIDGE 265

may have been, she always had her £20 regularly. It is interesting to see the weaver boy of Bally-naskeagh, who never received a lesson except from the Rev. Andrew Harshaw of Ballynafern, carrying off prizes for proficiency at Cambridge, and instructing others whose advantages must have been a thousand times superior to his own.

The educational arena is a great leveller of artificial and accidental distinctions. The name preceding Brontë's in the admission register is that of John Prettyman, son of the Venerable Archdeacon Dr. John Prettyman of Lincoln, and the name that follows Brontë's is that of Charles Sampson of Middlesex. Brontë's tutor was James Wood, who afterwards became master of St. John's.

As the handsome youth and distinguished scholar drilled shoulder to shoulder with his countryman, Lord Palmerston, and with the late Duke of Devonshire, few could have suspected his humble origin in Emdale, or the titanic struggle by which he had gained a foothold at the University.

Mr. R. T. Scott, the registrar of St. John's, has most kindly furnished me with all the information at his disposal. From the Term Register we learn that Patrick Brontë commenced residence on the 4th of October, 1802 ; kept the succeeding eleven University terms; took the B.A. degree the 23rd of April, 1806 ; and that his name was removed from the boards the 26th of May, 1808.

Mr. J. Willis Clarke, the registrar of the University, has furnished me with photographs of Brontë's matriculation and graduation signatures. The first was evidently written by the registrar, as

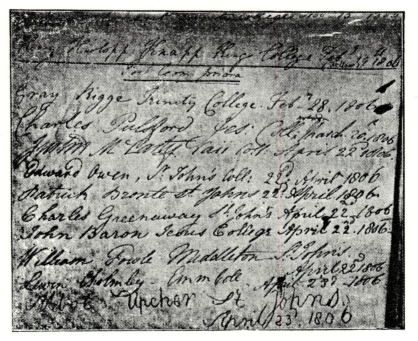

PATRICK BRONTË'S SIGNATURE ON PROCEEDING TO HIS DEGREE.

it is in the same handwriting as the three signatures that precede it. The second is Brontë's own writing, and I reproduce here the photograph of the page which contains it.

PATRICK BRONTË AT ST. JOHN'S, CAMBRIDGE 267

Patrick Brontë's footsteps have been so carefully traced, and his movements so fully accounted for, throughout the ecclesiastical by-ways of England, that I need not follow him beyond the walls of the University.* The ardent student was eclipsed in the country parson, but again appeared in the reflected light of his daughters.

* It has been persistently affirmed that Patrick Brontë ceased to visit his Irish home after he went to England; but, as I have already shown, the assertion is absolutely groundless. He was a visitor not only on holiday occasions, but in times of trouble. The only time I ever saw him was on one of his visits.

He preached one of his first sermons to his old friends and neighbours in Ballyroney Church. His youngest sister, Alice, told the Rev. J. B. Lusk of that sermon in the following words at their last interview : " Patrick came home after he was ordained, and preached in Ballyroney. All our friends and neighbours were there, and the church was very full. . . . He preached a gran' sermon, and never had anything in his han' the whole time " (*i.e.*, he had no manuscript).

CHAPTER XXVIII

THE IRISH BRONTËS AND "JANE EYRE"

THE Brontë novels were first read and admired in the Ballynaskeagh manse. This statement I am able to make with fulness of knowledge. *Jane Eyre* was read, cried over, laughed over, argued over, condemned to the lowest depths, exalted to the loftiest heights, by the Rev. David McKee and his brilliant children and numerous pupils, before the author was known publicly in England, or a single review of the work had appeared.

Were I not able definitely to settle this question now, the future historian would arrive at a very different conclusion. And I am myself able to submit documentary evidence which seems to prove in the most decisive manner the very opposite of what I have asserted. I have now in my possession a copy of the fourth edition of *Jane Eyre*, presented by Charlotte Brontë's father to Hugh, his eldest brother, apparently in the firm belief that the Irish Brontës had never seen the book.

The volume, which is considerably worn, contains an inscription worth quoting for many reasons. It is a memorandum in Patrick's hand, and it refutes the calumny that he forgot the old home after settling in England. It also reveals the price that Charlotte got for the copyright of her three novels; but it assumes that the uncles and aunts of the novelist had never seen the first editions of their

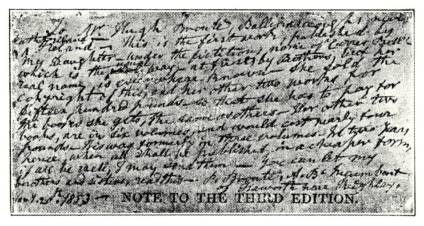

PATRICK TO HUGH REGARDING THE PRICE PAID FOR THE NOVELS.

niece's works. The memorandum which is written on the page over the "note to the third edition," is as follows:—

"To Mr. Hugh Brontë, Ballynaskeagh, near Rathfriland, Ireland.—This is the first work published by my daughter, under the fictitious name of 'Currer Bell,' which is the usual way at first by authors, but her real name is everywhere known.

THE BRONTËS IN IRELAND

She sold the copyright of this and her other two works for fifteen hundred pounds ; so that she has to pay for the books she gets, the same as others. Her other two books are in six volumes, and would cost nearly four pounds. This was formerly in three volumes. In two years hence, when all shall be published in a cheaper form, if all be well, I may send them. You can let my brothers and sisters read this.

" P. BRONTË, A.B.,
" Incumbent of Haworth, near Keighley.
"Jan. 20th, 1853."

At the time when Patrick Brontë sent to his old home the copy of the fourth edition of *Jane Eyre*, the Irish Brontës were already in full possession of the first editions of Charlotte's three novels. I have in my possession the copies of the three-volume first editions of *Shirley* and *Villette*, which they had in hand, and I distinctly remember the three volumes of the first edition of *Jane Eyre*, which I fear is now lost.

The explanation of this seeming difficulty is simple enough. In addition to the £500 * that

---

* It has been often said that Smith, Elder, & Co. paid a small annuity to the last of the Brontë aunts ; but this is not correct. An annuity of £20 per annum was granted by the Trustees of Pargeter's Charity on the representation of one of the Trustees, the Rev. D. Maginnis. The grant was made to Alice in March 1882, and lapsed with the death of the annuitant on the 15th of January, 1891.

THE IRISH BRONTËS AND "JANE EYRE" 271

Smith, Elder, & Co. paid Charlotte Brontë for the copyright of each of her novels, they would, as the custom is, allow her a number of copies for friends. They sent half a dozen copies direct to herself at first. The book was published on the 16th of October, and ten days later Charlotte acknowledged receipt of the copies in the following letter :—

                  " Oct. 26th, 1847.

" Messrs. Smith, Elder, & Co.
    " Gentlemen,—

      " The six copies of *Jane Eyre* reached me this morning. You have given the work every advantage which good paper, clear type, and a seemly outside can supply ; if it fails, the fault will lie with the author—you are exempt. I now await the judgment of the press and the public.

        " I am, gentlemen,
            " Yours respectfully,
                "C. BELL."

Charlotte Brontë's friends were not numerous, and she was most anxious that none of the few should find out that she was the author. In the distribution of even her six copies she would certainly send one to her friends in Ireland. Her father would be in absolute ignorance of the transaction, for though he wrote home regularly his brothers seldom wrote to him ; and hence the

THE BRONTES IN IRELAND

presentation of the copy of the cheap fourth edition, preserving to us the very precious inscription.

When the volumes arrived in Ireland there was no room for doubt as to the authorship of *Jane Eyre*. The Brontës had no other friend in England to send them books ; and even their friends would not have sent them great bulky expensive novels unless they were the authors of them themselves. The Brontës in Ireland neither wrote nor read romances. They lived them.

It was well known to the family that the clever brother in England had very clever daughters. Their habits of study, their wonderful compositions, their education in Brussels, were steps in the ascending gradation of the girls, minutely communicated by the vicar to his only relatives, and fairly well understood in Ballynaskeagh. Something was expected.

That something caused blank disappointment. C(urrer) B(ell) was a thin disguise for C(harlotte) B(rontë) ; but it did not deceive the relatives. Why concealment, if there were nothing discreditable to conceal? A very little reading convinced the uncles and aunts that concealment was necessary.

The book was not good, like Willison's *Balm of Gilead*, or like Bunyan's *Pilgrim's Progress*. It was neither history like Goldsmith, nor biography like Johnson, nor philosophy like Locke, nor

THE IRISH BRONTËS AND "JANE EYRE" 273

theology like Edwards; but "a parcel of lies, the fruit of living among foreigners."

The Irish Brontës had never seen a book like *Jane Eyre* before—three volumes of babble that would have taken a whole winter to read. They laid the work down in despair; but after a little Hugh resolved to show it to Mr. McKee, the one man in the whole district whom he could trust.

The reputation of his nieces in England was dearer to Hugh Brontë than his own.

He tied up the three volumes in a red handkerchief, and called with them at the manse. Contrary to his usual custom, he asked if he could see Mr. McKee alone. The interview, of which my information came from an eye-witness, took place in a large parlour which contained a bed and a central table, on which Mr. McKee's tea was spread out.

Hugh Brontë began in a low, mysterious whisper and with a regretful air to unfold his sad tale to Mr. McKee, as if his niece had been guilty of some serious indiscretion. Mr. McKee comforted him by suggesting that the book might not have been written by his niece at all. At this point Hugh Brontë was prevailed upon to draw up to the table to partake of the abundant tea that had been prepared for Mr. McKee, while the latter proceeded to examine the book.

Both gentlemen devoted themselves to the task in hand. Brontë settled down in the most self-denying manner to dispose of the heap of bread and butter and the pot of tea, while Mr. McKee went galloping over the pages of the first volume of *Jane Eyre*, oblivious of everything else but the fascinating story.

The afternoon wore on, and Brontë sat still at the table, watching the features of the reader, as they changed from sombre to gay, and from flinty fierceness to melting pathos.

When the servant went in to remove the tea-things and light the candles both men were sitting silent in the gloaming. Mr. McKee, roused from his state of abstraction, observed Brontë sitting by the *débris* and empty plates.

"Hughey," he said, breaking the silence, "the book bears the Brontë stamp on every sentence and idea, and it is the grandest novel that has been produced in my time"; and then he added, "The child Jane Eyre is your father in petticoats, and Mrs. Reed is the wicked uncle by the Boyne."

The cloud passed from Hugh Brontë's brow, and the apologetic tone from his voice. He started up as if he had received new life, wrung Mr. McKee's hand, and hurried away comforted, to comfort others. Mr. McKee had said the novel was "gran'," and that was enough for the Irish Brontës.

CHAPTER XXIX

THE AVENGER ON THE TRACK OF THE REVIEWER

THERE was joy in the Brontë house when Hugh returned, and reported to his brothers and sisters what Mr. McKee had said about *Jane Eyre*. They needed no further commendation, for they knew no higher court of appeal on such a matter ; nor was there. They had all been alarmed lest Charlotte had done something to be ashamed of ; but on Mr. McKee's approval, pride and elation of spirit succeeded depression and sinking of heart *

* The Rev. W. J. McCracken, an old pupil of the Bally-naskeagh manse, writes me on this point : "You have no doubt often heard Mr. McKee's opinion as to the source of Charlotte's genius. When Charlotte Brontë published one of her books, there was always an early copy sent to the uncles and aunts in Ballynaskeagh. As they had little taste for such literature, the book was sent straight over to our dear old friend Mr. McKee. If it pleased him, the Brontës would be in raptures with their niece, and triumphantly say to their neighbours, 'Mr. McKee thinks her very *cliver*.' I well remember Mr. McKee reading one of Charlotte's novels, and in his own inimitable way making the remark, 'She is just

275

THE BRONTËS IN IRELAND

Mr. McKee's opinion of *Jane Eyre* did not long remain unconfirmed. The reviews of the work which appeared in English magazines were quoted in the Newry paper, probably sent by Mr. McKee, and found their way quickly into the uncles' and aunts' hands.

The publication of the book created a profound impression generally. It was felt in literary circles that a strong nature had broken through conventional restraints, that a fresh voice had delivered a new message. Men and women paused in the perusal of the pretty, the artificial, the inane, to listen to the wild story that had come to them, with the breeze of the moorland and the bloom of the heather.

The tragic pathos of human passion, working out its destiny and doom, entranced and thrilled the

her uncle Jamie over the world. Just Jamie's strong, powerful direct way of putting a thing.'"

Mrs. McKee, writes me from New Zealand: "My husband had early copies of the novels from the Brontës, and he pronounced them to be Brontë in warp and woof, before 'Currer Bell' was publicly known to be Charlotte Brontë. He held that the stories not only showed the Brontë genius and style, but that the facts were largely reminiscences of the Brontë family. He recognised many of the characters as founded largely on old Hugh's yarns polished into literature. When *Jane Eyre* came into the hands of the uncles, they were troubled as to its character; but they were very grateful to my husband for his good opinion of its ability. He pronounced it a remarkable and brilliant work before any of the reviews appeared."

AVENGER ON THE TRACK OF REVIEWER 277

English-reading race. The self-evidencing simplicity of the narrative disarmed incredulity, and
the fit proportion maintained, between the things
said and the manner of saying them, disenchanted
prejudice and suspicion. There was no apparent
art, but sincere truth ; there was no palpable style,
but the mechanism of nature. The vehement
energy and tempestuous frankness were as real
as the lightning and the hurricane ; and the playful
fancy and glowing heart brightened and warmed,
like the sunlight silvering the leaves or silently
ripening the corn.

The tears were sad and joyless, but genuine ; the
smiles were brimful of mirth. Men and women
saw the smiles and the tears, as clearly as they saw
the summer-lit moor. And so exquisite was the
gift of thought blended with the art of artless
expression, that only the facts appeared in the
transparent narrative.

With a few memorable exceptions, the favourable
verdict of the press was not only hearty but
enthusiastic.

The *Times* declared *Jane Eyre* to be a " remarkable
production. . . . Freshness and originality, truth and
passion, singular felicity in the description of natural
scenery and in the analysation of human thought,
enable this tale to stand boldly out from the mass,
and to assume its own place in the bright field of
romantic literature."

The *Edinburgh Review* proceeded as follows : " For many years there has been no work of such power, piquancy, and originality. . . . From out the depths of a sorrowing experience, here is a voice speaking to the experience of thousands. It is a book of singular fascination."

It was reviewed in *Blackwood's Magazine* thus : " *Jane Eyre* is an episode in this workaday world ; most interesting, and touched at once by a daring and delicate hand. It is a book for the enjoyment of a feeling heart and vigorous understanding."

In *Frazer's Magazine* Mr. G. H. Lewes expressed his verdict : " The book closed, the enchantment continues ; your interest does not cease. Reality, deep, significant reality, is the characteristic of the book. It is autobiography—not perhaps in the naked facts and circumstances, but in the actual suffering and experience. This gives the book its charm : it is soul speaking to soul ; it is utterance from the depths of a struggling, suffering, much-enduring spirit ; *suspira de profundis.*"

Tait's Magazine declared : " *Jane Eyre* has already acquired a standard renown. The earnest tone, deep fervour, and truthful delineation of feeling and nature displayed in its pages must render it a general favourite."

The *Examiner*, the *Athenæum*, and the *Literary Gazette* followed in the same strain ; while the

Daily News spoke with qualified praise, and only the *Spectator*, according to Charlotte, was " flat."

The club coteries paused, and the literary log-rollers were nonplussed, and Thackeray sat reading instead of writing.

The interest in the story was intensified, inasmuch as no one knew whence had come the voice that had stirred all hearts, or the hand that had led them out to see heights and depths in lowly lives undreamt of before.

Nor did the interest diminish when the mystery was dispelled. On the contrary, it was much increased when it became known that the author was not one of the great literary fraternity, who had assumed an *alias* to escape from the restraints of custom ; but a little, shy, bright-eyed, Yorkshire maiden of Irish origin, who could scarcely reach up to great Thackeray's arm, or reply unmoved to his simplest remark.

The Irish Brontës read the reviews of their niece's book with intense delight. To the uncles and aunts the pæans of praise were successive whiffs of pure incense. They had never doubted that they themselves were superior to their neighbours, and they felt quite sure that their niece Charlotte was superior to every other writer. The praise bestowed upon her was her due, and as it reflected some lustre on themselves they treasured it in their hearts.

THE BRONTËS IN IRELAND

But the Brontës were not content to enjoy silently their niece's triumph and fame. It is difficult to carry the full cup with steady dignity. Their hearts were full, and overflowed from the lips. The silent, self-contained Brontës had reached the period of their decadence, and as they had begun to imbibe a good deal of whiskey they were often heard boasting of the illustrious Charlotte. Sometimes even they would read to uninterested and unappreciative listeners scraps of praise cut from the Newry papers, or supplied to them from English sources by Mr. McKee. The whole heaven of Brontë fame was bright and cloudless; suddenly the proverbial bolt fell from the blue.

The *Quarterly* onslaught on *Jane Eyre* appeared, and all the good things that had been said by the other great magazines were forgotten. The news travelled fast, and reached Ballynaskeagh almost immediately. The neighbours who cared little for what the *Times*, *Frazer*, *Blackwood*, and such periodicals said had got hold of the *Quarterly* verdict in a very direct and simple form. The report went round the district like wild-fire, and it became the common talk that the *Quarterly Review* had said Charlotte Brontë, the vicar's daughter, was a bad woman, and an outcast from her kind.

The neighbours of the Brontës had very vague ideas as to what the *Quarterly* might be; but I am

AVENGER ON THE TRACK OF REVIEWER 281

afraid the one bad review gave them more piquant pleasure than all the good ones put together. There is a tendency in human nature to resent the sudden rise to eminence of near neighbours and common acquaintances. That they have reached fame and you have not is sufficient proof that all is not as it should be.

In the changed atmosphere the uncles and aunts assumed their old unsocial and taciturn ways. When their acquaintances came, with simpering smiles, to sympathise with them, their gossip was cut short by the Brontës, who judged rightly that the sense of humiliation pressed lightly on their comforters.

In their sore distress they went to Mr. McKee. He was able to show them the review itself. The reviewer had been speculating on the sex of Currer Bell, and, for effect, assumed that the author was a man ; but, he added, " whoever it be, it is a person who, with great mental power, combines a total ignorance of the habits of society, a great coarseness of taste, and a heathenish doctrine of religion. For if we ascribe the work to a woman at all, we have no alternative but to ascribe it to one who has, for some sufficient reason, long forfeited the society of her own sex."

Mr. McKee's reading of the review and words of comment gave no comfort to the Brontës. I am afraid his indignation at the cowardly attack only served to fan the flame of their wrath. The sun of his sympathy, however, touched their hearts, and their pent-up passion flowed down like a torrent of lava.

The uncles of Charlotte Brontë always expressed themselves, when roused, in language which combined simplicity of diction with depth of significance. Hugh was the spokesman. White with passion, the words hissing from his lips, he vowed to take vengeance on the traducer of his niece. The language of malediction rushed from him, hot and pestiferous, as if it had come from the bottomless pit, reeking with sulphur and brimstone.

Mr. McKee did not attempt to stem the wrathful torrent. He hoped that the storm would exhaust itself by its own fury and be followed by a calm, or that the outburst would clear away the dregs of anger, as a charge of gunpowder, exploded in the flues of the copper, scatters the accumulated soot.

But in the case of Hugh Brontë the anger was not a mere thing of the passing storm. The scoundrel who had spoken of his niece as if she were a strumpet must die. Hugh's oath was pledged, and he meant to perform it. The brothers recognised the work of vengeance as a family duty. Hugh had simply taken in hand its execution ; and though his brothers and sisters were moody and silent, they felt that the Brontë honour was safe in the hands of the Avenger.

AVENGER ON THE TRACK OF REVIEWER 283

Hugh Brontë set about his preparation with the calm deliberation befitting such a tremendous enterprise. Like Thothmes the Great, his first concern was with regard to his arms. Irishmen at that time had one national weapon. What the blood mare is to the Bedawi, or his sling was to King David, that was the shillelagh to Hugh Brontë the Avenger.

Irishmen have since proved their superiority as marksmen with long range rifles, and they have always had a reputation for expertness at "the long bow"; but the blackthorn cudgel has always been the hereditary weapon around which their affections were entwined, and at the touch of which their courage rose.

The shillelagh was not a mere stick picked up for a few pence, or cut casually out of the common hedge. Like the Arab mare, it grew up to maturity under the fostering care of its owner, and in the hour of conflict it carried him to victory.

The shillelagh, like the poet, is born, not made; though, like the poet, it is developed and polished. Like the poet, too, it is a choice plant, and its growth is slow.

Among ten thousand blackthorn shoots, perhaps not more than one is destined to become famous; but one of the ten thousand appears of singular fitness among its gnarled companions. As soon as discovered it is marked and dedicated for future service. Everything that might hinder its well-balanced development is removed from its vicinity, and any offshoot likely to detract from the perfect growth of the main stem is skilfully cut off. With constant care it grows thick and strong, and the bulbous root can be shaped into a handle which in an emergency can be used as a club.

Hugh Brontë was a man who looked before and hastened slowly. In early life he planted two oak trees by the edge of the Glen to supply wood for his coffin. They have become large trees, and they were pointed out to me by the nearest neighbour, Mr. Christopher Radcliffe, on the occasion of my last visit to the Brontë Glen.

Hugh had for many years been watching over the growth of a young blackthorn sapling, as if it had been an only child. It had arrived at maturity about the time the diabolical article appeared in the *Quarterly*. The supreme moment of his life had arrived, and the weapon on which he depended was ready.

Hugh Brontë returned home from the manse with his whole heart and soul set on avenging his niece. His first act was to dig up the blackthorn carefully, so that he might have enough of the thick root to form a lethal club. Having pruned it roughly, he placed the butt end in warm ashes night after night to season. Then when it had become sapless and hard he reduced it to its final

AVENGER ON THE TRACK OF REVIEWER. 285

dimensions. Afterwards he steeped it in brine, or " put it in pickle," as the saying goes ; and when it had been a sufficient time in the salt water, he took it out and rubbed it with shamois and train oil for hours. Then came the final process. He shot a magpie, drained its blood into a cup, and with the lappered blood polished the blackthorn till it became glossy black with a mahogany tint.

The shillelagh was then a beautiful, tough, formidable weapon, and when tipped with an iron ferrule was quite ready for action. It became Hugh's trusty companion, esteemed and loved for its use as well as for its beauty. No Sir Galahad ever valued his shield, or trusted his spear, as Hugh Brontë cherished and loved his shillelagh.

When the shillelagh was ready, other preparations were quickly completed. Hugh made his will by the aid of a local schoolmaster, leaving everything of which he was possessed to his maligned niece ; and then, decked out in a new suit of broadcloth in which he felt stiff and awkward, he departed on his mission of vengeance.

He set sail from Warrenpoint for Liverpool by a vessel called the *Sea-Nymph*, and walked from Liverpool to Haworth. His brother James had been over the route a short time previously, and from him he had received all necessary directions as to the way. He reached the vicarage on a Sunday when all, except Martha the old servant, were at church. At first the faithful old Yorkshire woman looked upon him as a tramp, and refused to admit him into the house; but when he turned to go down to the church, road-stained as he was, she saw that the honour of the house was involved, and she agreed to allow him to remain till the family returned. Under the conditions of the truce, he was able to satisfy Martha as to his identity, and then she rated him soundly for journeying on the Sabbath day.

Hugh's reception at the vicarage was at first chilling; but soon the girls gathered round him, and inquired about the Glen, the Knock Hill, Emdale Fort, and the Mourne Mountains, but especially with reference to the local ghosts and haunted houses. On all these topics Hugh had much to say that not only confirmed what they already had heard, but stimulated their curiosity to hear more.

Hugh was bitterly disappointed to find his niece so small and frail. His pride in the Brontë superiority had rested mainly on the thews and comeliness of the family, and he found it difficult to associate mental greatness with physical littleness. On his return home he spoke of the vicar's family to Mr. McKee as "a poor *frachther*," a term applied to a brood of young chickens. He did not babble of such matters, except to the one man whom he knew he could trust. From his brother

AVENGER ON THE TRACK OF REVIEWER 287

Jamie, Hugh had heard that Branwell had something of the *spunk* he had expected from the family on English soil ; but he was too small and fantastic, and a chatterer, and could not drink more than two glasses of whiskey at the Black Bull without making a fool of himself. In fact, Jamie, during a visit, had to carry Branwell home more than once from that refuge of the thirsty.*

The declaration of Hugh's mission of revenge was received by Charlotte with incredulous astonishment. But gentle Anne sympathised with him, and wished him success. Had it not been for Anne's enthusiastic encouragement, Hugh would have returned straight home from Haworth in disgust.

Patrick, as befitted a clergyman, condemned the undertaking, and did what he could to amuse Hugh, and to draw his mind from its fierce intents. He was careful that Hugh's entertainments should be to his taste, and he took him to see a prize fight. His object was to show him "a battle that would take the conceat out of him." It had the contrary effect. Hugh thought the combatants were too fat and lazy to fight, and he always asserted that he could have "licked them both."

---

* Rosey Heslip, a cousin of Charlotte Brontë, told the Rev. J. B. Lusk that she heard her mother say that Jamie, on his return from England, declared "that Charlotte had eyes that looked through you."

THE BRONTËS IN IRELAND

The vicar also took him to Sir John Armitage's, where he saw a collection of arms, some of which were exceedingly unwieldy. Hugh was greatly impressed with the heaviness of the armour, and especially with Robin Hood's helmet, which he was allowed to place on his head. He admitted that he could not have worn the helmet or wielded the sword; but he maintained at the same time that he " could have eaten half a dozen of the men he saw in England "—in fact, taken them like a dish of whitebait.

When Hugh Brontë had exhausted the wonders of Yorkshire, to which the vicar looked for moral effect, he started on his mission to London. A full and complete account of his search for the reviewer would be most interesting, though somewhat ludicrous; but the reader must be content with the scrappy information at my disposal.

Through an introduction from a friend of Branwell's, he found cheap and suitable lodgings with a working family from Haworth. They lived near the river. As soon as Hugh had got fairly settled, he went direct to John Murray's publishing house and asked to see the reviewer. He declared himself an uncle of Currer Bell, from whom he had come direct, and he said he wished to give the reviewer some specific information.

He had a short interview at Murray's with a man who said he was the editor of the *Quarterly*, and

AVENGER ON THE TRACK OF REVIEWER 289

who may have been Lockhart ; but Hugh told him he could only communicate to the reviewer his secret message.

He continued to visit Murray's under a promise of seeing the reviewer ; but he always saw the same man, who pressed him greatly to say who Currer Bell was.

Hugh declined to make any statement except into the ear of the reviewer ; but as the truculent character of the avenger was probably very apparent, his direct and bold move did not succeed. They ceased to admit him at Murray's.

Having failed at Murray's, he went to the publishers of *Jane Eyre*, and told them plainly he was the author's uncle, and that he had come to London to chastise the *Quarterly Review* critic. They treated him civilly without furthering his quest ; but he got from them an introduction to the reading-room of the British Museum and to some other reading-rooms.

In the reading-rooms he was greatly disgusted to find how little interest was taken in the matter that absorbed his whole attention. He met, however, one kind old gentleman in the British Museum, who thoroughly sympathised with him, and took him home with him several times. On one occasion he invited a number of people to meet him at dinner. The house had signs of wealth such as he had never before seen or dreamt of. Everybody was kind to him. After dinner he was called on for a speech, and when he sat down they cheered him and drank his health.

They all examined his shillelagh, and before parting promised to do their best to aid him in discovering the reviewer; but his friend afterwards told him at the Museum that all had failed, and that they considered Hugh's undertaking hopeless.

He tried other plans of getting on the reviewer's track. He would step into a bookshop, and buy a sheet of paper on which to write home, or some other trifling object. While paying for his small purchase he would take up the *Quarterly Review*, and casually ask the bookseller who wrote the attack on *Jane Eyre*.

He always found the booksellers communicative, if not well-informed. Many told him the absurd story then current connecting *Jane Eyre* with Thackeray. None of them seemed able to bear the thought of appearing ignorant of anything. It was quite well known, they assured him, that Thackeray had written the review; "in fact, he had admitted that he was the author of the review."

Some declared that Mr. George Henry Lewes was the author; others said it was Harriet Martineau; and some even assured him that Bulwer Lytton, or Dickens, was the critic. These names were given with confidence, and with circumstantial details which seemed to create a probability;

AVENGER ON THE TRACK OF REVIEWER 291

but his friend whom he met daily at the Museum assured him that they were only wild and absurd guesses.

Hugh Brontë failed to find the reviewer of his niece's novel, but in his earnest quest he explored London thoroughly. He saw the Queen, but was better pleased to see her horses and talk with her grooms.

He saw reviews of troops, and public demonstrations, and cattle shows, and the Houses of Parliament, and ships of many nations, that lay near his lodging; and he visited the Tower, and other objects of interest; and when his patience was exhausted and his money spent, he returned to Haworth on his homeward journey.

Thus ended one of the strangest undertakings within the whole range of literary adventure.

His stay at the vicarage was brief. During his absence consumption had been rapidly sapping the life of the youngest girl. The house was gloomed with bereavement and dismal with forebodings, and yet the gentle Anne received him with the warmest welcome, and talked of accompanying him to Ireland, which she spoke of as "home." At parting she threw her long, slender arms round his neck, and called him her noble uncle; and the great giant felt amply rewarded for his fruitless efforts, and never after referred to the circumstance without his eyes filling with tears. Charlotte took him for a walk on the moor, asked a thousand questions, told him about Emily and Branwell, and slipping a few sovereigns into his hand, advised him to hasten home. On the following day he parted for ever from the family that he would have given his life to befriend.

No welcome awaited him at home, because he had failed in his mission. He gave to Mr. McKee a detailed account of his adventures in England ; * but I do not think any other stranger ever heard from him a single word regarding the sad home at Haworth.

---

* A daughter of Mr. McKee's told me that more than once she tried to get this story from Hugh Brontë at first hand, but always in vain. He would talk freely enough about what he had seen in England, but grew silent, and dangerous-looking, when pressed as to the subject of his journey. On one occasion she said she had already heard the story from her father. He looked vexed, as if his secret had been betrayed, but he simply replied, "Then you don't need to hear of it from me." I often talked with Hugh of his adventures in England, but the conversation always came to an abrupt termination if I referred to Haworth, or the object of his mission.

Jamie's visit to Haworth may have been before the publication of *Jane Eyre*, but it took place during the time that Branwell was drinking himself into the grave. Hugh's visit was a little before the death of Anne. For prudential reasons, Hugh's mission was at first kept secret, and after its failure pride would not permit a reference to it. The adventure was known only to Mr. McKee, and the brothers and sisters at home. Those who were not at home never heard of it.

CHAPTER XXX

WHO WROTE THE REVIEW? A WORKING HYPOTHESIS

THE December number of the *Quarterly Review* of 1848 is perhaps the most famous of the entire series. Its fame rests on a mystery which has baffled literary curiosity for close on half a century. "Who wrote the review of *Jane Eyre*?" is a question that has been asked by every contributor to English literature since the critique appeared; but up till September last year the question was asked in vain, and all guesses were wide of the mark.

The descendant and namesake of the eminent projector and proprietor of the *Quarterly* does not feel at liberty to solve the mystery by revealing the writer. I admire the loyalty of John Murray to a servant whose work has attained an evil pre-eminence. It is interesting to know in these prying and babbling times that in the house of Murray the secret of even a supposed ruffian is safe to the third generation.

THE BRONTËS IN IRELAND

Like the fracturer of the Portland vase, and the assassins of eminent men who have gained notoriety in connection with the greatness that they sought to destroy, the *Quarterly* reviewer is inseparably linked with *Jane Eyre*, on account of the diabolical attempt to shatter the novel and blast the character of its author. The pretence of religion and morality under which the dastardly deed was attempted has given point to the detestation with which it has been regarded ; and even now the reviewer is looked on with something like hatred as a common enemy. The verdict of condemnation with regard to the review has been unanimous, and sentence has been passed on the unknown criminal in language anything but judicial.

Mrs. Gaskell referred to the article as " flippant," and added : " But flippancy takes a graver name when directed against an author by an anonymous writer ; we call it then cowardly insolence." Then she closes a long-drawn-out rhetorical passage, calling on the reviewer to " pray with the publican rather than judge with the Pharisee."

Swinburne, in his *Note on Charlotte Brontë*, deals with the review in a passage which is without a parallel in the English language :—

" It is of infinitely small moment that we know only by its offence the obscure animal now nailed up for this offence by the ear, though not by name, —its particular name being as undiscoverable as

WHO WROTE THE REVIEW? 295

its generic designation is unmistakable,—to the undecaying gibbet of immemorial contempt.

"When a farmer used to nail a dead polecat on the outside of his barn door, it was surely less from any specific personal rancour of retaliatory animosity towards that particular creature than by way of judicial admonition to the tribe as yet untrapped, the horde as yet unhanged, which might survive to lament if not to succeed the malodorous malefactor. No mortal can now be curious to verify the name as well as the nature of the typical specimen which then emitted in one spasm of sub-human spite at once the snarl and the stench proper to its place and kind.

"But we know that from the earlier days of Shelley onwards to these latter days of Tennyson, whatsoever things are true, whatsoever things are honest, whatsoever things are just, whatsoever things are pure, whatsoever things are lovely, whatsoever things are of good report, become untrue, dishonest, unjust, impure, unlovely, and ill-famed, when passed through the critical crucible of the *Quarterly Review.*"

Mr. Augustine Birrell's *Life of Charlotte Brontë* is worth reading for his onslaught on the reviewer. He drops on "the base creature" as "the detestable hypocrite who wrote the review in the *Quarterly.*" He refers to "the male ruffianism" of the reviewer who recognised the "tragic power" and "moral sublimity" of the book; "yet mindful of his bargain, true to his guineas," he sought, by circulating what he himself calls "the gossip of Mayfair," to destroy the reputation and fair fame of the author. Mr. Birrell concludes as follows :—

"If it be said that such nauseous and malignant hypocrisy as that of the *Quarterly* reviewer ought not to be republished : the answer is, that it is impossible to rejoice with due fervour over exterminated monsters until we have gazed in museums upon their direful features. It is a matter of congratulation that such a review as the one we have quoted from is now impossible. It is also convenient that the name of the reviewer is unknown, so that no one can arise and say, ' I loved that man !'

"It was judgments like those of the reviewer that tempted people to forswear respectability altogether—to break up house, and live in the tents of Bohemia—since remaining respectable and keeping house exposed them to the risk of meeting, actually meeting, the reviewer himself and other members of his family."

Who was "the detestable hypocrite" and "base creature"? Or how did the "male ruffianism" take form? I believe I am able now to show that these matters are no longer secrets.

There is nothing clearer to my mind than that the composition of the article is the work of different

WHO WROTE THE REVIEW? 297

hands. Of the thirty-two pages of the review three
or four pages stand like bits of drugget set into
a Persian carpet, or like patches of Paisley on a
Cashmere shawl. The difference between fustian
and silk is not greater in substance, texture, and
tone, than that which exists between the original
article and the interpolations, which were intended
to make it palatable to conventional and commonplace minds. The scissors as well as the pen were
used in bringing the original review to the required
standard, and one can only wonder that certain
parts were allowed to stand.

The notorious article deals with three subjects,
but chiefly with *Vanity Fair* and *Jane Eyre.* The
reviewer begins with *Vanity Fair*, which fairly
takes his breath away. He is lost in admiration :
" We must discuss *Vanity Fair* first, which, much
as we were entitled to expect from its author's pen,
has fairly taken us by surprise." The novel is
dealt with as a work up to the reviewer's standard.
He writes about it in the measured style of a censorious man of the world. He lauds Becky Sharpe,
but he hands her over to destruction with a light
heart. He compares her to one of Bunyan's
pilgrims, " only," he adds, " unfortunately this one
is travelling the wrong way. And we say unfortunately merely by way of courtesy, for in
reality we care little about the matter." She is an
admirable piece of art, but that her back is turned

to heaven and her face towards hell is only a matter for pleasantry.

Having thus jauntily handed Becky Sharpe over to reprobation without compunction or regret, the critic tells us : " She came into the world without the customary letters of credit upon the two great bankers of humanity, heart and conscience ; and it was no fault of hers if they dishonoured all her bills. All she could do in this dilemma was to establish the firmest connection with the inferior commercial branches of sense and tact, who secretly do much business in the name of the head concern, and with whom her fine frontal development gave her unlimited credit. . . . She practised the arts of selfishness and hypocrisy like everybody else in *Vanity Fair*, only with this difference, that she brought them to their highest possible pitch of perfection. . . . At all events, the infernal regions have no reason to be ashamed of little Becky, nor the ladies either ; she has at least all the cleverness of her sex."

Becky and her sex having been thus disposed of, and Thackeray sufficiently lauded, the censorious man of the world has a sarcastic fling at the " stern moralist " and the reader of " good books " :—

" Poor little Becky is bad enough to satisfy the most ardent student of ' good books.' Wickedness beyond a certain pitch gives no increase of gratification even to the sternest moralist ; and

WHO WROTE THE REVIEW?

one of Mr. Thackeray's excellencies is the sparing quantity he consumes."

"Upon the whole," he adds, "we are not afraid to own that we rather enjoy her *ignis-fatuus* course, dragging the weak and vain and the selfish through much mire after her, and acting all parts, from the modest rushlight to the gracious star, just as it suits her, clever little imp that she is."

The reviewer turns from *Vanity Fair*, which he has found up to his taste, with its pack of reprobates, to *Jane Eyre*, and the character, style, and tone of the article changes. The nonchalant Gallio of morals suddenly becomes a "stern moralist."

The style becomes mixed. In one of the first sentences there is an interpolation, throwing the sentence off its balance, and necessitating specific illustration, which is done by a feeble hand. Two hands are now at work on the composition—a pagan hand, and a would-be Christian. Here is a good specimen. The reviewer, speaking of Jane Eyre after her great disappointment, thus proceeds :—

"A noble, high-souled woman, bound to us by the reality of her sorrow, and yet raised above us by the strength of her will, stands in actual life before us. . . . *Let us look at her in the first recognition of her sorrow after the discomfiture of her marriage. True it is not the attitude of a*

300 THE BRONTËS IN IRELAND

Christian who knows that all things work together for good to those who love God ; but it is a splendidly drawn picture *of a natural heart,* of high power, intense feeling, and fine religious instinct, falling prostrate, but not grovelling before the blast of sudden affliction."

Let the reader go through this passage, first omitting the part in italics, which are mine, and then read the whole with the italics, and he will see how the jumble is made up.

The styles are as different as the sentiments, but the pagan hand is clearly the stronger. If internal evidence as to styles is admissible, in this case it is overwhelming and decisive.

But the case is much stronger as regards diversity of sentiment. It is so patent that it requires no finding out. It has not to be brought to light, it stands revealed. Could the parts in italics have been written by the frivolous pagan who cheered Becky Sharpe with courtesy, but without care, on her way to the bottomless pit, and who jeered at the "stern moralist" and the reader of "good books" only a few pages earlier? If the question cannot be satisfactorily settled by the parts already quoted, let us read what follows :—

"We have said that this was a picture of the natural heart. This, to our view, is the great and crying mischief of the book. Jane Eyre is throughout the personification of an unregenerate and

WHO WROTE THE REVIEW? 301

undisciplined spirit—the more dangerous to exhibit from this prestige of principle and self-control, which is liable to dazzle the eye too much for it to observe the insufficient and unsound foundation on which it rests. It is true Jane does right, and exerts great moral strength ; but it is the strength of a mere heathen mind, which is a law unto itself. No Christian grace is perceptible upon her. She inherited in fullest measure the worst sin of our fallen nature, the sin of pride. Jane Eyre is proud, and therefore she is ungrateful too. It pleased God to make her an orphan, friendless, and penniless ; and yet she thanks nobody, least of all the friends, companions, and instructors of her helpless youth, for the food and raiment, the care and education vouchsafed to her, till she was capable in mind and fit to provide for herself. Altogether the autobiography of Jane Eyre is preeminently an anti-Christian composition. There is throughout it a murmuring against the comforts of the rich and the privations of the poor, which, so far as each individual is concerned, is a murmuring against God's appointment. There is a proud and perpetual asserting of the rights of man for which we find no authority in God's Word or in His providence. There is that pervading tone of ungodly discontent which is at once the most prominent and the most subtle evil which the law and the pulpit, which all civilised society has, in fact, at the present day to contend with. We do not hesitate to say that the tone of mind and thought which has overthrown authority, and violated every code—human and Divine—abroad, and fostered charterism and rebellion at home, is the same which has written *Jane Eyre*."

It is not necessary to say whether the judgment expressed in this passage is correct or not. It is enough for my purpose to point out that it is entirely out of harmony with all that has gone before in the *Review*, and still more in direct conflict with all that comes after. The entire passage is an interpolation.

The reviewer who was fascinated with Becky Sharpe, who had neither heart nor conscience, and of whom "the infernal regions had no reason to be ashamed," could hardly be the same who deplores Jane Eyre's "natural heart" and "unregenerate spirit," lack of grace and gratitude, fulness of pride and original sin.

There are three or four pages only of this kind of stuff, and then for the remaining nine pages of the article the reviewer is in full accord with Jane Eyre, and pleads with great earnestness for the better treatment of governesses.

He dwells on their qualifications, their troubles, the fictitious barriers raised between them and their employers, "the perpetual little dropping-water trials," all of which embitter the lives of these

WHO WROTE THE REVIEW? 303

ill-used ladies, whom the servants detest, and the children may love, but not befriend.

But the reviewer goes farther. He who was supposed to have declared *Jane Eyre* pre-eminently an anti-Christian composition, "on account of the assertion of the rights of man and discontent with poverty," becomes guilty of the very thing he was supposed to have denounced on the previous page. He strikes out fiercely at the Christian mothers who take advantage of destitute ladies' helplessness to pay them starvation wages :—

"There is something positively usurious in the manner with which the misfortunes of the individual are nowadays constantly taken advantage of to cut down the stipend of the governess to the lowest ratio which she will accept."

The same article which declared God's Word and Providence on the side of wealth, and condemned discontent in misery, goes far beyond *Jane Eyre* in democratic discontent and socialistic levelling. Charlotte Brontë, with her Tory sentiments and democratic instincts, simply removes the mask from the face of hypocrisy. The work of Wellington's little adorer is made into a bogey, and held up as the spirit responsible for revolution abroad, for charterism and rebellion at home ; but a few pages farther on the bogey is forgotten, and the language of the review far outstrips "the tone of mind and thought" of the little Tory governess.

THE BRONTËS IN IRELAND

On the part of the reviewer there is no mere lifting of the veil from the face of hypocrisy. He goes direct for the transgressors. " That service, not the abundance of supply of female labour, should be the standard of pay," is the canon which he lays down. But he declares, "The Christian parent lowers the salary because the friendless orphan will take anything rather than be without a situation."

" This," he exclaims, " is more oppressive than the usurious interest of the money-lender, because it weighs not upon a selfish, thoughtless, and extravagant man, but upon a poor, patient, industrious woman."

The reviewer has here dropped the flippant tone and become fiercely in earnest. He almost flies in the face of constituted authority. " Workmen may rebel, tradesmen may combine," but the poor friendless governess is left to the uncovenanted mercies of the English matron.

The simple explanation of these inconsistencies is this. The reprobated article was written with a generous appreciation of *Jane Eyre*, which the writer recognised as the work of a "great artist"; but the passages that are out of harmony with the article were inserted by the editor or by his instructions.

Lockhart was editor of the *Quarterly* at the time, and he was responsible for " the tone of mind

WHO WROTE THE REVIEW? 305

and thought " of the articles that were inserted. Propriety in the eyes of the *Quarterly* readers was outraged by the manner in which the new hand had broken through the crusts of things held sacred, and hence the three or four pages out of thirty-two, of maudlin sentimentality and insincere philistinisms.

There was nothing unusual in such treatment of articles in those days. The ablest writers of the time were obliged to submit to such editing. Southey and Thackeray, and even Carlyle, had their works pared and polished and padded to suit the demands of the public taste.

A magazine was a commercial speculation, and it was the duty and business of the editor to shape its contents to please the reader and profit the proprietor.

If my hypothesis * is right, it matters little who wrote the article, though there is no longer any secret with regard to the matter. In wealth of knowledge, felicity of expression, appreciation of good work, and lofty superiority of tone, it is in

---

* Since the above was in type Mr. Andrew Lang has written me that he "accidentally came across the *Quarterly Review*, and saw at once that the article was interpolated." He also informs me that he published his views on the subject in the *Daily News* some time in 1889-92. He generously adds : "I don't want to boast of my priority of discovery, but the coincidence increases the probability that we are right."

the main a typical *Quarterly* article. But with all its excellence, it would have been forgotten had not the sugary, vinegary, watery morsel been inserted in the middle of it.

The question, then, " Who supplied the palatable pabulum to the *Quarterly*?" admits of but one answer. The entire responsibility lies at Lockhart's door ; and whether the work was done by his sub-editor, or by Elwin, or by his own hand, the blame in future must be considered his, and his alone. Nor need we use again, in this connection, such phrases as "spiteful and malignant hypocrisy." It is not likely that there was anything either spiteful or malignant in the matter. In fact, it was largely a business transaction of supply and demand. The editor merely did what he was expected to do, and what under the circumstances he was used to do.

Assuming the editor's responsibility for the incriminated interpolations, who wrote the article itself ? Secrets are having a bad time of it in our day, and the authorship of the article is no longer a secret. As has been generally suspected, the writer was a woman, and that woman was Miss Rigby, the daughter of a Norwich doctor, and better known as Lady Eastlake.

The well-kept secret was brought to light by Dr. Robertson Nicoll in the *Bookman* of September 1892. Dr. Nicoll found the key to the

WHO WROTE THE REVIEW?

mystery in a letter written on the 31st of March, 1849, by Sara Coleridge to Edward Quillinan, Wordsworth's son-in-law, and published in the *Memoirs and Letters of Sara Coleridge.** The following is the passage in Sara Coleridge's letter referring to the matter :—

"Miss Rigby's article on *Vanity Fair* was brilliant, as all her productions are. But I could not agree to the concluding remark about governesses. How could it benefit that uneasy class to reduce the number of their employers, which, if high salaries were considered in all cases indispensable, must necessarily be the result of such a state of opinion?"

The *Quarterly* article on *Vanity Fair* dealt also with *Jane Eyre* and with the *Report of the Governesses' Benevolent Institution* for 1847, and it is without doubt the article referred to by Sara Coleridge.

On this matter Sara Coleridge was not likely to be under any mistake. Miss Rigby was her intimate friend, and not likely to conceal from her so important a literary event as the production of a *Quarterly* review. Besides, Sara Coleridge had private information regarding the *Quarterly*, for in the same letter she says, "I am awaiting with some curiosity the arrival of the *Quarterly*, in which Mr. Lockhart has dealt with Macaulay."

* Vol. ii., p. 223.

THE BRONTES IN IRELAND

I am also informed that Mr. George Smith, the publisher of *Jane Eyre*, declares without hesitation or doubt that he had always known that Lady Eastlake was the author of the *Quarterly* article, and that he had declined to meet her at dinner on account of it.

The fact that the brilliant Miss Rigby was the writer of the review greatly strengthens my interpolation theory. To me it seems beyond the range of things probable, that the pharisaic part of the article could have come from the same source as *Livonian Tales* and the *Letters from the Shores of the Baltic*.

The article is therefore of a composite character. It was written by Miss Rigby the year before her marriage with Sir Charles Lock Eastlake.

I know it will be said that the genial Lockhart would not have added the objectionable fustian to the superior material supplied by Miss Rigby ; but I repeat that it lay with him as a mere matter of business, and a purely editorial affair, to maintain the traditional tone of the *Review*.

Printed in the United Kingdom
by Lightning Source UK Ltd.
119334UK00002BA/4